FOR UNTO US A SON IS GIVEN

A Close Look At
The Biblical Foundation For
The Messiahship Of Jesus

by

Martin Fromm

Copyright 1998
Martin Fromm
All Rights Reserved

ISBN: 0-7392-0205-7

Printed in the USA by

MORRIS PUBLISHING
3212 East Highway 30 • Kearney, NE 68847 • 1-800-650-7888

DEDICATION

This book is dedicated to my beloved sister who, to the best of my knowledge, never made a profession of faith in Jesus. Nevertheless, she lived by a higher standard than most, and was the finest example of Godly virtue, decency and humanity that I had ever met. Her kindness, sense of humor, and dedication to all she undertook, serve as an inspiration to me and to all who knew her.

In loving memory of

DORIS P. FISS

ACKNOWLEDGEMENTS

A special note of thanks is due Martin and Lois Scharfglass (The Marlowe Group) for the many hours they spent in helping me to make this book readable. Their diligence in editing, correcting and formatting - and generally holding my feet to the fire - is gratefully acknowledged.

There are others, too numerous to mention, who have impacted my life, and brought me to this point. However, special thanks to Clara and Joe Rubin for years of instruction, example and friendship.

PREFACE

There have been many books written about the messiahship of Jesus, most of which show the harmony between the Hebrew Scriptures (usually referred to as the Old Testament) and the New Testament. No doubt there is a beautiful correlation in comparing the writing of the Hebrew prophets to the glorious fulfillment found in the New Testament. However, Jewish people do not generally accept the validity of the New Testament, so this book attempts to prove its point by presenting the gospel solely from the Hebrew Bible.

Paul, and the other apostles (most, if not all of whom, were Jews), did not have the New Testament, and they obviously used only the sacred Hebrew scriptures to prove Jesus' identity. It is hoped that the same logic will prevail in this book. Not only will such a presentation be a more meaningful testimony to Jewish readers, but it may provide our Gentile readers with some helpful hints on how to present Jesus to a Jewish audience which is not inclined to view the New Testament as authoritative.

This book will also examine many of the arguments offered by Jewish sources in refuting the claims of Christianity. Simply declaring the Jewish eyes to be spiritually blind or unenlightened fails to acknowledge how well-thought-out and reasonable the objections of Judaism can be. We must not only be more aware of these challenges, but explore these rebuttals to better understand the true application of the scriptures that are controversial.

On a personal note, the points of view offered by some very eloquent and informed Jewish critics have brought the writer to a heightened awareness of Biblical truth, and a rejuvenation of faith that had, to some degree, been taken for granted. Compelling arguments forced me to look deeper into the Word and provided new insights and a joyful reacquaintance with passages that were instrumental in my coming to faith in Jesus many years ago.

INTRODUCTION

It is difficult, if not impossible, to divorce oneself from deep-rooted convictions. As such, it would be presumptuous to call this undertaking an objective look at Jesus' credentials in support of His being the promised Messiah of Israel. I've lived with this conviction for about thirty years.

The conclusions I reached did not come overnight. My earlier years were spent in disbelief, and I argued passionately against what seemed to be an absurdity - Jews accepting Jesus as their Savior.

This book attempts to look at the Biblical passages dealing with this subject with a non-jaundiced eye. Trying to be as fair as possible, the Masoretic (Hebrew) text (The Twenty-Four Books of the Holy Bible, Hebrew and English, Carefully Translated After the Best Jewish Authorities, by Isaac Leeser, Hebrew Publishing Co., 77-79 Delancey St., NYC) is used for most of the controversial material, and is indicated by "MT" after the citation. In an attempt to avoid the allegation that a "Christian" translation puts a different slant on these passages, the King James Bible was used in the non-controversial areas, or where there were no marked differences between the two. Words and phrases not commonly used in English appear in *italics*, and are listed alphabetically in the glossary.

The intent of the book is in no way to ridicule or diminish Jewish scholarship, which is deeply respected by the author. Rather, it is hoped and prayed that eyes will be opened to alternative understandings, even as mine were, thirty years ago.

CONTENTS

DEDICATION		ii
ACKNOWLEDGEMENTS		iii
PREFACE		iv
INTRODUCTION		v
1	A STONE OF STUMBLING	/ 1
2	THE KINSMAN IN THE FLESH	/ 10
3	THE PROPHET LIKE MOSES	/ 26
4	THE SUFFERING SERVANT	/ 33
5	THE PLURALITY OF GOD	/ 56
6	THE SEVENTY WEEKS OF DANIEL	/ 70
7	THE OVERVIEW OF MESSIAH'S CAREER	/ 80
8	PSALM 45	/ 99
9	THE FEASTS OF JEHOVAH	/ 110
10	THE TIME OF JACOB'S TROUBLE	/ 141
11	LAW OR GRACE	/ 145
EPILOGUE		/ 154
GLOSSARY		/ 157
ABOUT THE AUTHOR		/ 163

1

A STONE OF STUMBLING

A series of unusual but Divinely-appointed circumstances resulted in some prolonged dialogue with Orthodox Jews who are involved in anti-missionary activity. To my surprise, these conversations left me with the impression that Messianic Judaism (the faith shared by Jewish people who accept Jesus as Israel's Messiah) shares many of the same views as traditional Judaism, and we are not as far apart as originally supposed. While there are serious obstacles, there is a good representation of Biblical passages and concepts where we are in agreement. Why, then, is there such passionate disagreement and even hostility?

Although the roots of Christianity are embedded in Judaism, as more and more Gentiles embraced the teachings of Jesus, accommodation was made for pagan customs and practices which had nothing to do with Biblical precepts. When the Gentiles began to predominate, Jewish influence diminished and criticism heightened against Judaism for having rejected Jesus. Anti-semitism, with satanic support, began to take root, and over the course of the years the rift developed into a chasm. Nominal Christianity, more concerned with church doctrine than Biblical truth, fanned the flames of hostility, resulting in an emphasis of the differences in spite of the doctrines held in common.

The icing on the cake was added by some church fathers whose diatribes against Jewish people had a profound influence upon the multitudes. Not receiving Jewish support in promoting their brand of Christianity, men like Martin Luther laid a foundation for condemnation and intolerance. The Jewish populace now were perceived as Christ-killers, anti-Christian and unworthy of the grace of God. To complicate matters, well-intentioned Christians, due to lack of knowledge and limited understanding of the Jewish mindset and customs, inadvertently engendered more distrust.

It was only a matter of time when the less subtle approaches gave way to forcible conversions, crusades and *pogroms*. Present day ecumenicism, based upon compromise and accommodation, is viewed by Judaism as reverting to the more subtle approach of using deceit and deception where coercion has failed. In summation, meaningful dialogue is difficult when there is such distrust and lack of objectivity.

Having stated all this, it would appear to be all but impossible for Jewish people to come to faith in Jesus. We must remember, however, that God, in His sovereign will and infinite mercy, remains in control and will accomplish His objectives. Although human frailties and gross wickedness were designed with evil intent, the ultimate truth will ever be that "...all things work together for good to them who love God..." The Creator of all life used the rejection of Jesus by the Jew as the means through which the nations would come to believe on Israel's Messiah. At the same time, the prophetic Word would enhance our faith and elevate our respect for the wonders of the living God Who sees the beginning and the end.

Let us begin with a look at the rejection of Jesus. Is this evidence of His being an imposter, or is it fulfilled prophecy? A careful examination of God's Word will show that the events that unfolded are recorded in advance so that we would see the hand of God.

Consider, for example, Moses' exhortation before his death, as recorded in Deuteronomy 32. Israel was severely chastised for having forsaken the one true God and lapsing into idolatry. They "...lightly esteemed the Rock of his [their] salvation" (v. 15), and "Of the Rock that begat thee thou art unmindful, and hast forgotten God that formed thee" (v. 18), grew complacent and provoked God to anger. Thus, the Lord indicated that He would hide His face from them as a people without faith. The prophecy continues: "They sacrificed unto devils, not to God; to gods whom they knew not, to new gods that came newly up, whom your fathers feared not...They have moved me to jealousy with that which is not God; they have provoked me to anger with their vanities: and I will move them to jealousy with those which are not a people; I will provoke them to anger with a foolish nation" (vs. 17, 21).

Clearly, the pagans, the aliens who were not privy to the covenants and oracles of God, were to be provocateurs in arousing the jealousy of God's called-out nation. Historically, we now see how many of the Jewish nation have come to believe through the prayers, earnest witness and faithfulness of the "foolish" Gentiles. It is no coincidence that whereas Israel over the centuries has followed numerous false messiahs, the Gentiles did not fall prey to these deceptions. On the other hand, the true Messiah, of whom Moses and the prophets testified, was the only Redeemer received by the Gentiles. The very program predicted here by Moses serves as evidence that the Gentiles were to be the instrument through which Israel would come to faith in the Messiah initially rejected.

Isaiah admonished Israel (chapter 8:13-15): "Sanctify the Lord of hosts himself; and let him be your fear, and let him be your dread. And he shall be for a sanctuary; but for a stone of stumbling and for a rock of offence to both the houses of Israel, for a gin and for a snare to the inhabitants of Jerusalem. And many among them shall stumble, and fall, and be broken..." So Jesus' rejection, rather than rendering His credentials invalid, confirms the preordained plan of God.

Add to this Psalm 118, which reveals that: "The stone which the builders refused is become the head stone of the corner. This is the Lord's doing; it is marvellous in our eyes." In Isaiah 8:16, Israel was told that God has laid in Zion a tried stone, a precious stone, in Whom they were to trust. Yet, the testimony will ever be that Israel lightly esteemed the Rock that begot them.

Prophecy dealing with Israel's rejection of their Messiah is found as well in Psalm 110:1-3: "The Lord [Jehovah] said unto my Lord, Sit thou at my right hand, until I make thine enemies thy footstool. The Lord shall send the rod of thy strength out of Zion: rule thou in the midst of thine enemies. Thy people shall be willing in the day of thy power..."

Several points are worthy of our consideration. Jehovah is addressing someone the psalmist, David, calls his Lord. Who is David's Lord? Traditional Judaism would have us believe this psalm is talking about David, but David is speaking of his Lord who will come into power. This ruler is invited by Jehovah to sit at His right hand (a place reserved for a coequal) in heaven, until those described as "thy people", who are at enmity with Him, would become His footstool, or be compliant upon His return in power.

We are fortunate that, in retrospect, we know Jesus, having been rejected and crucified, ascended to the right hand of the Father where He awaits the time to return in power. For the present, examining these verses suggests that the one David calls Lord came into the presence of the Hebrew nation ("thy people"), since this contact would have been necessary to result in rejection and alienation.

Confirmation is seen in Hosea 5:15. He carries forward this theme of rejection, ascending to God and awaiting the time to return: "I will go and return to my place, till they acknowledge their offense, and seek my face: in their affliction they will seek me..."

Israel has been guilty of many offenses, but the singular overriding error is having rejected their Savior. This is further borne out in Zech. 12:10, where it is declared that God would pour out the spirit of grace and supplication upon the house of Israel and the house of Judah, and they "...shall look upon me [him] whom they have pierced, mourn for him, as one mourneth for his only son, and be in bitterness for him, as one in bitterness for his firstborn." The initial rejection is followed by remorse when the nation finally realizes its mistake.

There are two incidents mentioned in the scriptures that elicit the same understanding. The first account is described in Exodus 17:6: "Behold, I will stand before thee there upon the rock in Horeb; and thou shalt smite the rock, and there shall come water out of it, that the people may drink..." The second time, somewhat different instructions were provided (Numbers 20:7-10): "And the Lord spake unto Moses, saying, Take the rod, and gather thou the assembly together, thou, and Aaron thy brother, and speak ye unto the rock before their eyes; and it shall give forth his water, and thou shalt bring forth to them water out of the rock: so thou shalt give the congregation and their beasts drink."

Moses proceeded to smite the rock twice with his rod, and water came out in abundance. But because of smiting, and not speaking to the rock as instructed, the Lord said to Moses and Aaron: "...Because ye believed me not, to sanctify me in the eyes of the children of Israel, therefore ye shall not bring this congregation into the land which I have given them" (Num. 20:12). In spite of Moses' illustrious career and exemplary service, this act prohibited him from entering the land of promise.

What initially appears to be quite puzzling is consistent with the subject under consideration. Israel rejected the rock of their salvation, and was to pay the consequences. The Lord's preordained plan was to be smitten in his first coming, but in the second advent, Moses was instructed to speak to the rock to bring forth the water. And so, Jesus was smitten and bore the reproach the first time. In His second coming in power, this is not the case, and smiting or rejecting Him the second time is not acceptable.

The initial rejection, followed by a change of heart, occurs at two separate points in time. Whether or not this appeals to our sense of logic is unimportant, for God alone dictates the means through which His objectives will be realized. The fact remains that the spiritual blindness of Israel is the means by which the door is opened to the Gentiles who, in turn, will provoke Israel to emulation.

Prophetic utterances continue to reveal how this divine program is to unfold. In Genesis 49:1, Jacob calls his sons together for a look at what is to take place "...in the last days". Our attention is particularly drawn to Judah, who is to have a vital role in Israel's restoration. Verse 10 lays this foundation: "The sceptre shall not depart from Judah, nor a lawgiver from between his feet, until Shiloh come; and unto him shall the gathering of the people be."

The scepter is the symbol of kingship and authority. It is generally understood from this that the tribe of Judah was to remain in power until the coming of the anointed one. Some see "Shiloh" as the name of Messiah, or a symbolic name pointing to Him. The name implies peace, from the root, *shalom.* Per Isaiah 9:6, one of Messiah's names is Prince of Peace.

Interpretation is somewhat obscure because the Hebrew manuscripts, unlike the English language, are written without vowels. As such it is also conjectured that the letters here *(SHLO)* are the word *shelo,* which actually is understood to be "of whose it is" or, in effect, "to whom it belongs".

All of Israel's kings were seated on the throne of God, and were only occupying that throne on a temporary basis in God's stead. The One whose right it is, Messiah, was to come to Israel before the power to rule was removed from Judah.

It is only logical to conclude that Messiah was to come prior to 70 C.E., at which time Judah's control was overthrown and Jerusalem destroyed. In the ninth chapter of Daniel this sequence is confirmed. Messiah was to appear while the Temple stood, be "cut off", and the Temple would be rebuilt at a later time. Suffice to say, prophecy demands that Messiah was to appear prior to Judah's downfall, and the general rejection of Jesus by Judaism in no way invalidates the prophecy. If anything, the denial of Jesus is consistent with the scriptures, and sets the stage for His later return in power, leading to His acceptance.

Jacob's prophetic vision not only called for the continuance of the Davidic dynasty, but "...unto him shall the gathering of the people be". This too compels us to look for a second coming to accomplish that which remains unfulfilled. Judaism is understandably skeptical, since Jesus did not satisfy the messianic prediction that world peace would prevail when Messiah comes. When the two comings are kept in view we can better understand what took place. We will address this in a more detailed manner when we explore the timetable established in Daniel's prophecy of the "seventy weeks".

There are rabbinical commentaries that similarly suggest two comings of the Messiah. The lives of Moses and Joseph, for instance, are seen as prototypes, foreshadowing the career of Israel's Redeemer. Moses was raised as the son of Pharaoh, seated in a position of great authority and possessing great wealth. Joseph was also the son of a man of great substance, and enjoyed a favored status. Incidents in both their lives resulted in a reversal of fortune, disappearance from view, and the return to authority and power for the purpose of redemption. We are to understand that, just as Moses and Joseph returned from obscurity to deliver the nation, in like manner Messiah will come a second time to restore Israel.

Jesus, the only begotten of the Father, left his position of prominence, abandoning heaven to accomplish God's purpose on earth. In His humanity He was crucified, disappeared from view, but we await His return to complete His preordained role. This is more than speculation, as we've already seen in those Biblical passages which speak of His rejection and ascension. The prophecies of Hosea and Zechariah will bear out that we will acknowledge our offense, seek His face, and receive the spirit of grace and supplication. It is only a matter of time, known at this point to God alone.

The concept of two comings, as stated, is not believed or accepted by traditional Judaism. In order to reconcile the problems engendered by those passages which speak of Messiah's rejection and death, and seem to contradict His ushering in a universal reign of peace, the Jewish expositors popularized the theory that there are two messiahs. One is to be the suffering servant as described by Isaiah, and the other, our triumphant deliverer and restorer of peace. One is from the house of David, and the other from the house of Joseph.

The two-messiah theory is supported by a *Chanukah haftorah*, *Parshat Vayeishev*, which begins in Genesis 37, opening with the word *Vayeishev*, or "And he lived" or "dwelled". These passages deal with two of Jacob's sons, Joseph and Judah. Two eternal stories of redemption are allegedly revealed; one through the matriarch Leah, and the second through the matriarch Rachel. It has been conjectured that since Leah was given to Jacob in marriage through

Laban's deceit, her role embodies cosmic events which are inscrutable and defy logic.

On the other hand, Rachel personifies God's sovereignty and open manifestation. The events involving Rachel are clear and open, whereas those involving sister Leah are part of God's mysteries.

From these two, God was preparing a messiah from the house of David and a messiah from the house of Joseph. Each was to make a contribution to the eternity of the nation of Israel. The Talmudical passages which comment on these chapters add that the light of messiah is created in *Vayeishev*, but in the end, the two will blend, and they will herald a single redemption. We are informed by the *Zohar* that Judah and Joseph must be joined into one, for Joseph is the *tzadik* (righteous) and Judah the king, and these brothers bring good and peace into the world.

When Jacob finally sends Judah to Egypt to rejoin Joseph, the scripture says he was sent to Goshen. The Hebrew letters, "G-S-H-N", are the same letters that appear on the traditional *Chanukah dreidel*, but arranged N-G-H-S: an acronym for *Ness Gadol Hayah Shom*. The declaration is: "A great miracle happened there." This was the miracle of the reunification of the brothers and the renewal of the oneness of the nation.

There are many godly servants who have been used to deliver Israel, and Joseph here is a prime example. His life in many ways is symbolic of the ultimate Savior. We saw how these parallels include starting from a position of prestige and authority, falling into obscurity and reappearing to play a role in redemption. Add to this being the innocent sufferer, not compromising Godly values, and remaining uncomplaining in service. Yet there is nothing in the word of God that suggests the Messiah is to be any other than the One from the house of David.

Joseph's life may provide understanding as to the role of Messiah, but the only true Redeemer is from the house of David. In fact, Psalm 78:67-68 addresses this question beyond any doubt: "Moreover he refused the tabernacle of Joseph, and chose not the tribe of

Ephraim: But chose the tribe of Judah, the mount Zion which he loved."

Some commentators tell us that there is a potential messiah born in every generation, ready to reveal himself under the proper circumstances. The timing is generally tied in to the worthiness of the nation. The emphasis is always that of a human, not divine, savior, most frequently described as a prophet like Moses. The critics agree that God can do anything He chooses, including manifestation in the flesh, but why would He choose such a course? A number of reasons can be cited to satisfy that question which will be discussed in the next chapter.

2

THE KINSMAN IN THE FLESH

Levitical law provides for redemption in the person of a *goel*, or kinsman-redeemer; that is, a near relative in the flesh who thus has the right and responsibility usually associated with raising up seed in the name of the deceased. In the story of Judah, as unfolded in the *Chanukah sedra* to which we referred, Judah had two sons, Er and Onan. Both of them were declared to be evil and were slain by God. Judah promised his remaining son, Shelah, to his widowed daughter-in-law, Tamar. However, not fulfilling this promise, we read that Tamar took matters into her own hands. She played the harlot in seducing Judah and gave birth to twins, Pharez and Zarah.

Perhaps this rather sordid account of Judah's less-than-exemplary life popularized the theory of a second and more worthy messiah, Joseph. If we were left to our own devices, we must conclude that Joseph was by far a better example of holy living. Let's not forget as well that Joseph was the son of Rachel, the choice of Jacob, and his true love. But let us not forget also that God did not ask us to vote for the messiah of our choice.

The better-known example of the kinsman-redeemer is taken from the Book of Ruth. This widow of Elimelech's and Naomi's son, although a Moabitess, refused to leave her widowed mother-in-law. Her famous and oft-quoted words are as inspiring and meaningful today as when she first declared, "...whither thou goest, I will go; and where thou lodgest, I will lodge: thy people shall be my people, and thy God my God..." (Ruth 1:16).

Returning to Bethlehem of Judea, Ruth providentially was sent to glean wheat in the fields of Boaz, a kinsman of the deceased, Elimelech. Here, too, we see the hand of God Who made provision in the law for the sustenance of the needy. Leviticus instructs that the corners of the harvest were to be left for the widow and orphan.

Ruth's virtue and character were well-reported. She was obedient in following Naomi's instructions. The story unfolds to explain that Boaz must first offer Ruth in marriage to a closer relative. Although this kinsman had the right of redemption, he declined so as not to mar his own inheritance. This paved the way for Boaz who had both the right and the desire to act as the *goel*, and to raise up seed in the name of the departed.

The book of Ruth closes with this genealogy: "Now these are the generations of Pharez: Pharez begot Hezron, And Hezron begat Ram, and Ram begat Amminadab, And Amminadab begat Nahshon, and Nahshon begat Salmon, And Salmon begat Boaz, and Boaz begat Obed, And Obed begat Jesse, and Jesse begat David" (4:18-22). Lineage to Messiah is established, and made possible by the *goel*.

The law made provision for a kinsman-redeemer. It required that he be a close relative in the flesh. To fulfill the law, God took on flesh, becoming our Redeemer and near-relation. As in the case of Boaz, Jesus had both the right and desire to act in this behalf, and without regard to the personal cost. Boaz was the great-grandfather of David, and Jesus' lineage is traceable to him. Another reason for Messiah to come while the Temple was standing is that His genealogy could be established. The records were maintained in the Temple, and there could be no question with regard to the validity of His lineage.

The scriptures impose even greater difficulty. Redemption required not only a near-kinsman, but don't forget that atonement requires a spotless or sinless offering. This opens up a Pandora's box, because so much controversy surrounds the subject of Leviticus 17:11. The life of the flesh is in the blood, and was to be offered upon the altar for the remission of sins. A much more detailed look is warranted. But for now, let us consider that since an Eternal God, Who is Spirit, cannot be sacrificed on the altar, it necessitated manifestation in the flesh to satisfy this provision of the law.

There is a tremendous philosophical difference of opinion, since Judaism argues that man can be righteous, and yet sin. A most eloquent argument along these lines may appeal to some, but the preponderance of scripture does not bear this out. Over and over again we are reminded "...there is not a just man upon earth, that doeth good, and sinneth not" (Ecc. 7:20). Isaiah (64:6) adds that "...all our righteousnesses are as filthy rags", and 1 Kings 8:46 declares: "...there is no man that sinneth not..." Jeremiah (17:9) explains: "The heart is deceitful above all things, and desperately wicked: who can know it?"

We learn from David in Psalm 51 that we, like him, are shaped in iniquity, and conceived in sin from the womb. We spend millions of dollars to educate, and emphasize ethical behavior and responsibility, all to no avail. Not a single cent has to be spent to teach how to deceive or cheat. The sin nature is revealed in that mere babies lie without the benefit of coaching or training. Based upon the Biblical standard, then, we must come to realize that God alone could accomplish what was impossible for man with an inherent sin nature.

We have read many rabbinical sources that agree with what is now deemed to be "Christian" theology. Tradition teaches that we possess a *yetzer tov* and *yetzer harah* - a good and an evil nature. *Divrei Ha Yamim* ("The Words of The Days", known as the book of Chronicles) 6:38 assures us that "there is no man who will not sin." God thus declares (Is. 63:5): "And I looked, and there was none to help; and I wondered that there was none to uphold: therefore mine own arm brought salvation unto me..."

God's resolution of a most intricate problem was to offer Himself in the person of Jesus to do what man could not accomplish for himself. The "arm" of the Lord is understood to be salvation by Jewish commentators, and we will deal with this further to show that the "arm" is a person - Jesus. Suffice to say for the present, the scriptures make it clear that only God can forgive sin, only God can redeem man, only God is righteous. We must conclude: "...in the Lord our God is the salvation of Israel" (Jer. 3:23).

The sacrificial system teaches the same truth: the vicarious suffering of the spotless animal was the acceptable offering upon the altar. At the time of the exodus, when God called out His nation, each family was to take, examine and hold the Passover offering for three days, to be certain there was no spot or blemish. Nothing less than perfect was acceptable upon the altar. In like manner, Jesus was examined for three days, and Pilate's declaration was: "...I, having examined him before you, have found no fault in this man..." (Luke 23:14).

Even though it was the custom to release a prisoner, the crowd called for the crucifixion of Jesus and the release of Barrabas, a convicted murderer. Herod declared as well: "...nothing worthy of death is done unto him" (Lk. 23:15). God's promise was to exempt those from the penalty of death who killed the passover (sacrifice), and placed the blood on the doorposts and lintels. He declared that only when He sees the blood would they be spared. Thus, only the blood of Jesus, the spotless Lamb of God (and *Goel*), was acceptable by God's standard.

To conclude that Israel, clearly unrighteous and burdened with a sin nature, would be accepted as a vicarious atonement, is made even more untenable when you read Psalm 49:7-8: "None of them can by any means redeem his brother, nor give to God a ransom for him: (For the redemption of their soul is precious, and it ceaseth for ever...)". There isn't enough money to pay, and there isn't a human who qualifies as being innocent.

Israel was forewarned that their sin would result in severe punishment and that they would be scattered among the nations as a consequence of their apostasy. A holy God carried through accordingly. If Israel were guiltless, she would not have been punished by a holy God. Being justifiably punished for their sins, it is obvious that Israel could not have been an acceptable sacrifice.

On one hand it is apparent that by virtue of all being sinners, no man could be an atonement for another. Why, then, did the Lord ask Abraham to offer Isaac upon the altar? Isaac, and all born of the flesh, would not be acceptable, so was God contradicting Himself? Since this is not possible, we look for an object lesson.

Emphasis is made that Isaac was Abraham's only son, and once more we are given a prophetic picture of the price God was willing to pay in offering His only begotten. Isaac's life, therefore, foreshadows that of Messiah (as did Moses and Joseph), providing a hint as to what we might expect. He was the child of promise, the gift of God and in the messianic line.

Since Isaac was not a child at this time, he could easily have resisted his father's will. This points to a life of submission and obedience. When coming to Moriah, Isaac asked: "...where is the lamb for a burnt offering?" Abraham replied: "...My son, God will provide himself a lamb for a burnt offering..." (Gen. 22:7-8). It would have been simple and grammatically correct to respond that God would provide, but the Hebrew scripture reveals the insertion of "provide himself". This too was a clue that God, Himself, was to be the sacrificial Lamb who would vicariously suffer for the sins of the world.

Now we come to another seemingly insurmountable problem. Since all born in the flesh have an inherited sin nature, how could Jesus be born in the flesh and yet remain sinless? If He were the product of an earthly mother and father, He would have been disqualified like everybody else. But being born of a virgin without the benefit of man, whose seed would pass along the sin nature, resolves that dilemma.

Genesis 3:14-15 sets the stage in revealing that there was to be enmity between the serpent and the woman and between his seed and the woman's seed. Whereas Satan would bruise the heel (of this seed), the seed of woman would bruise his head. The Hebrew is more forceful, suggesting that his head would be crushed, or, in effect, be dealt the death blow.

Many traditional commentators expound that the seed of the serpent, or Satan, are the spiritually evil, whereas the seed of the woman are God's children. However, since it is clear that all born of woman have the sin nature, the triumphant seed of woman who defeats Satan is more appropriately the Messiah. He uniquely is the seed of woman, not the seed of man. This messianic interpretation is supported by the *Targum* Jonathan, where it is written that the Jewish community was to gain victory over the devil in the days of King Messiah.

An examination of Isaiah 7:14MT is helpful in understanding what may be considered to be a rather difficult concept: "Therefore will the Lord Himself give you a sign: behold, this young woman shall conceive, and bear a son, and she shall call his name Immanuel [God with us]."

I specifically quote the Hebrew scripture which uses the term "young woman", but further thought must be given to the accuracy of this rendering. As such, we must look at this prophecy in context.

Judah's king, Ahaz, was examining the water supply by "...the end of the conduit [aqueduct] of the upper pool..." (v. 3). The kings of Syria and Israel had formed a confederacy with the intent to dethrone Ahaz and set up a Syrian pretender, Tabael. The plan called for a siege against Jerusalem, and Ahaz was concerned about having an adequate supply of water. Isaiah records that "...his heart trembled, with the heart of his people, as the trees of the forest are shaken before the wind" (7:2).

The Lord sent Isaiah to encourage Ahaz and assure him that the plan to besiege the city would not succeed. In fact, before certain stages of growth were reached in the life of a child (Immanuel), Syria and Ephraim would no longer pose a threat. To strengthen his faith in the Lord, Isaiah added: "Ask thee a sign from the Lord thy God: ask it in the depth, or high up above" (7:11MT). Ahaz' response was: "I will not ask, and I will not tempt the Lord" (7:12MT). In truth, Ahaz was not trusting God, in spite of such a seemingly confident statement. He had already sought the help of Assyria to join in a league against the invading forces. This compels Isaiah to expose the hypocrisy by declaring: "...Is it too little for you to weary men, that ye will weary also my God?" (7:13MT). As such, the promise is that God Himself would give a sign, and, in fact, <u>be</u> the sign.

A sign or miracle is promised, but traditional Judaism does not concede that a miracle was to take place. Yet, the prophecy to offer a sign, in the heights above or depths below, would support the promise to be a miracle. Further, prefacing the promise with *hineh*, or "behold", reveals as well that an unusual occurrence was prophesied. A commonplace event, such as a woman giving birth, certainly would not qualify as a miracle, but the virgin birth provides a satisfactory explanation.

Jewish critics argue that the Hebrew *bethulah*, ordinarily translated as "virgin", is not used here. Rather, the word *almah*, which describes a young woman, is proof that this has nothing to do with a virgin birth. We can respond with confidence that the use of "virgin" is the sensible conclusion demanded by this passage.

Bethulah would represent a problem when you consider its usage in Joel 1:8, which states: "Lament like a virgin girded with sackcloth for the betrothed [husband] of her youth." The Hebrew *ba-al* is usually translated as "husband". It obviously presents difficulty for the translator, so he uses "betrothed". The normal usage reveals, however, that - as stated - a *bethulah* is not always a virgin. Since *bethulah* is obviously used for other than a virgin, as in this instance, God uses another word which appears seven times in the scriptures (*almah*). Each points specifically to a virgin. The use of "virgin" in these seven passages is consistent with the context in each instance.

Almah is used in Ex. 2:8 to describe Moses' unmarried sister, Miriam, who watches as Pharaoh's daughter discovers the baby Moses in the bulrushes of the Nile. The Hebrew translates *almah* as "maiden", although she is, beyond doubt, a virgin.

In the Song of Songs (1:2-3, 6:8) the plural form of *almah*, or *almos*, is translated as "maidens" or "young women". Reference is made to those who serve in the presence of the king, and had to be pure. Again, "virgins" would properly describe these chaste women.

The matriarch Rebekah, in Gen. 24:15-16, is called a virgin where *bethulah* is used, but in verse 43 of this same chapter she amazingly becomes "young woman" when *almah* is used. Did she suddenly lose her virginity, or is it appropriate to claim that *almah* legitimately describes a virgin?

A rather obscure passage in Proverbs 30:18-19 again translates *almah* as "young woman". The writer states that there are four things too wonderful, or which cause him to wonder: the way of an eagle in the air, the way of a serpent on a rock, the way of a ship on the sea and the way of a man with an *almah*. The common thread in all these sights that cause wonder or uncertainty is that each is unfathomable and unpredictable. It is not possible, in viewing these scenes, to guess what direction will be taken. Will the eagle fly up or down, veer right or left? Will the serpent strike, and from which direction? As the ship disappears over the horizon, will it go left or right? What will happen between the man and the maid; will she fall prey to temptation?

If she were not a virgin, the question would be superfluous. Certainly, the author of Proverbs would not categorize these as "things that I know not". The use of "virgin" gives proper sense to this passage.

In a discussion with an Orthodox Jew, the argument was presented that the four things in common are that none would leave a trace. He pointed out that the next verse (30:20) supports this conclusion: "Such is the way of an adulterous woman; she eateth, and wipeth her mouth, and saith, I have done no wickedness." The implication is that *almah* can refer to an adulterer. Obviously, this is intended to suggest that Mary was not a virgin, but an adulterous woman.

There is no support for such interpretation, and all students of the language will agree that *almah* is at least a young woman of marriageable age. The argument that leads to this conclusion is suspect as well. Whereas an eagle and a serpent would not leave a trace, this is not true of a ship on the ocean. A wake is left for hours after a ship's passing, and is evidence of its having been present long after passing.

An honest appraisal, I believe, requires us to see the parallelism in the explanation I gave. An adulterous woman who professes to have done no wrong can in no way be likened to an *almah*. The only wonder she may cause is how she could delude herself into believing that she had done no wrong!

When the Hebrew scriptures were translated into Greek in what is known as the Septuagint, the word *parthenos* was employed, which is equivalent to "virgin". This translation, significantly, was the collaboration of 70 Greek-speaking rabbis. As we consider the concept of the virgin birth, we cannot ignore other verses which are consistent with this understanding. Genesis 3, generally regarded as being messianic, reveals that our ultimate hope comes from the *zerah shel eshah*, or "the seed of woman". Although the scriptures consistently reckon genealogy from the male, Messiah is uniquely understood to be the woman's seed. Other passages which speak of the coming of a messiah similarly draw attention to the woman and her womb.

Per Psalm 22, which many realize describes the crucifixion scene, it is stated in vs. 9-10: "But thou art he that took me out of the womb: thou didst make me hope when I was upon my mother's breasts. I was cast upon thee from the womb: thou art my God from my mother's belly."

In another passage regarded as messianic, Micah (5:1MT) speaks of the ruler to be born in the nondescript town of Bethlehem of Judea: "...whose origin is from olden times, from most ancient days"; and he will be "...great even unto the ends of the earth..." (v. 3MT), and bring peace. In verse 2MT of this chapter, once again the reference is: "Therefore will He give them up, until the time that she who travaileth hath brought forth..." Two additional times in Isaiah (49:1-5) reference is made to being called from the womb and being formed in the womb to be God's servant. It is no accident that Messiah comes from woman, not man, and that "virgin" specifically excludes male participation.

Discussion on this issue usually prompts the question as to why the name of Jesus is omitted from the Hebrew scriptures, if all this indeed were true. Rather than attempting to answer for God, we can consider that it is "...the honor of kings to search out a matter"

(Prov. 25:2MT). A hint is provided in that the Hebrew word *yeshua* means salvation, and this is the Hebrew equivalent of the Greek name, Jesus.

Moreover, Is. 49:1 provides an even more important clue: "...The Lord hath called me from the womb; from the bowels of my mother hath he made mention of my name." It would seem, therefore, to avoid speculation as to His identity, Messiah was not to be named until His being formed in the womb of the virgin. This, incidentally, was the point at which the angel of God appeared to Mary and told her to call the child Jesus, because He was to be the salvation (*Yeshua*) of Israel.

There are still two major objections to what we see here as referring to the virgin birth of Jesus. First, there is no outward physical manifestation accompanying virginity, so it would not qualify as a sign. Secondly, how would a birth that is not to take place for several centuries be a sign to Ahaz? The insistence that a sign be overtly visible is not necessarily true. Jewish law understood that it was impossible to determine a woman's virginity by merely looking at her. Provision, therefore, was made in the law to deal with potential deceit by an impure woman. This statute was also intended to protect an innocent party wrongfully accused of being unchaste. The tokens of virginity (the blood upon the bedsheet used on the wedding night) was to be kept as evidence, and could be presented if the question arose. Thus, a sign could very well be spoken about in advance of presenting physical evidence to establish its validity.

This still leaves the question regarding a birth which would not take place for more than 600 years, being offered as a word of comfort to Ahaz. His fear was the imminent invasion by Syria and Israel, and it is argued that it is inconceivable that the prophecy of Jesus' birth would make sense in this context.

Let us remember that God, through the prophet Isaiah, first reassures Ahaz that he would see Syria and Israel destroyed (Is. 7:8). Then the prophet addresses "O house of David" (v. 13). This sign, then, was for all of Judah, not for Ahaz alone. It was an indication that the Davidic dynasty was to remain in existence until the coming of Messiah. Such an assurance by far exceeded the mere survival of Jerusalem against the impending invasion, for it was pointing to the perpetuation of the nation for a far more lasting period.

It is well worth adding that the Hebrew "*ha alma*", literally "the virgin" or "this virgin", points to a specific individual, of whom the Hebrew nation would have knowledge. In essence, it points not merely to "a" person, but a specific individual to whom other references have been made. The "virgin" is thus linked to the one previously spoken of, the *zerah shel eshah*, "the seed of the woman".

Having presented these scriptural references to support the virgin birth, we now must confront traditional Judaism's objections to the alleged inconsistency of Jesus' lineage. This is further complicated by the prophetic message in Jeremiah 22:30: "Thus saith the Lord, Write ye this man childless, a man that shall not prosper in his days: for no man of his seed shall prosper, sitting upon the throne of David, and ruling any more in Judah."

Frankly, this not only poses a problem for the Hebrew-Christian but for the Jewish people as well. If we are to understand that Messiah is to come from the seed of David, the tribe of Judah, how do we circumvent this curse upon Jeconiah? Fortunately the virgin birth provides a solution (but not for our spiritually unenlightened Jewish brothers). Only one born of a virgin has not inherited the sin nature passed on by man's seed.

Matthew's genealogy (Matt. 1) traces the regal line through Joseph, who is included in the Solomonic branch, and reveals that Josiah begot Jeconiah (or Coniah), and that Jacob begot Joseph, the husband of Mary. Joseph makes Jesus a descendant of David through Jeconiah. The controversy surrounding a different genealogy used by Luke is explained by realizing that he traces the royal line through David's son, Nathan. Luke is actually showing Mary's genealogy, which is not the regal line (since it does not include the male), but makes Jesus a descendant through both Mary and Joseph.

In this instance we see Joseph called the son of Heli, and not the son of Jacob, as referenced by Matthew. Obviously, Joseph did not have two fathers, but rather, Heli is his father-in-law (Mary's father). Being Mary's husband he can correctly be addressed as the son of Heli. In fact, whereas the terminology in Matthew is "Jacob begat Joseph", Luke informs us that Joseph is the son of Heli (not "begotten of") (Luke 3:23-38).

The marriage of Joseph and Mary puts Joseph, who was in the regal line to the throne, into the royal line as well. Thus, by virtue of this marital relationship, Jesus has the legal right to the throne. At the same time, not being a direct descendant of Jeconiah, since He is not the physical son of Joseph, the prophecy of Jeremiah is not violated.

Being married prior to the birth of Jesus made Joseph a legal father, and Jesus a true descendant, but not <u>direct</u> descendant of Jeconiah. The right to the throne is established, yet He remains free of the curse that was invoked upon Jeconiah. The sin nature passed along by man's seed was never inherited by Jesus, the child of the Holy Spirit and the virgin.

Messiah is referred to as "Immanuel", God with us, in the seventh chapter of Isaiah. Chapter 9 further develops the understanding we are meant to have of His identity. The chapter opens making reference to the lands of Zebulun and Naphtali, and then to Galilee, all of which were vexed or afflicted. Due to a lack of spiritual light, the prophet says that the inhabitants of these territories were in darkness and dwelling in the land of the shadow of death. Now the light was to shine upon them.

In essence, where the darkness is greatest, the need is most evident, and the light was to come to these areas in the person of Israel's Messiah. This light would bring great joy likened to the joy of the harvest. Deliverance would follow along with spiritual victory as was experienced "in the day of Midian" (Is. 9:4).

The reference here is to Gideon's supernatural defeat of the Midianites. From an army of 32,000, God had Gideon set apart a small band of 300 to destroy Midian, which would make His divine intervention clear to all (Judges 7). Here, in Isaiah 9:6, the Lord is revealing how great victory is to be wrought by God, "For unto us a child is born, unto us a son is given: and the government shall be upon his shoulder: and his name shall be called Wonderful, Counsellor, The mighty God, The everlasting Father, The Prince of Peace."

These names and attributes are clearly divine and give weight to the understanding that, although manifested in the flesh, Messiah is not of human origin. While there are ample examples in scripture where men are called by names of God, the usage here is unique. This is no ordinary naming of a child who hopefully will meet a parent's expectation as exemplified by that name. Rather, we are given a string of appellations that describe God alone, and which are ascribed by God Himself.

Due to the christological implications, translators insert the word "of" so that it reads: "Wonderful, Counsellor of the Mighty God...of the Everlasting Father..." Not only is this tampering with the intent of the passage, it does not satisfy the purpose it is meant to serve. It would be contradictory and unbiblical to address any human being as God's counsellor. As the heavens are above the earth, so are His ways above ours, and past searching out. We can cite many appropriate verses which put this into perspective, such as Job 5:9MT, which exclaims: "Who doeth great things which are unsearchable, marvellous things till they are without number..." According to Is. 40:28, "...there is no searching of his understanding"; and, in 41:28 he adds: "For I beheld, and there was no man; even among them, and there was no counsellor, that, when I asked of them, could answer a word." Who, then, can qualify as the counsellor to a great and mighty God Who constantly confounds, and is not bound to perform in accordance with our limited understanding? God has no counsellor.

Further attesting to the divine origin of the Child to be born, Isaiah states: "Of the increase of his government and peace there shall be no end, upon the throne of David, and upon his kingdom, to order it, and to establish it with judgment and with justice from henceforth even for ever. The zeal of the Lord of hosts will perform this"

(Is. 9:7). No mere human being could perform such a herculean task: to guarantee absolute justice and perfection throughout eternity. Only the Mighty God and Everlasting Father could accomplish such a feat.

In the second verse of the fourth chapter of Isaiah we are introduced to Messiah as the Branch of the Lord, who shall "...be beautiful and glorious, and the fruit of the earth shall be excellent and comely for them that are escaped of Israel." This theme is continued in 11:1, where we learn: "And there shall come forth a rod out of the stem of Jesse, and a Branch shall grow out of his roots..."

Supernatural qualities are ascribed to Him: "And the spirit of the Lord shall rest upon him, the spirit of wisdom and understanding, the spirit of counsel and might, the spirit of knowledge and of the fear of the Lord...and he shall not judge after the sight of his eyes, neither reprove after the hearing of his ears: But with righteousness shall he judge the poor, and reprove with equity for the meek of the earth: and he shall smite the earth with the rod of his mouth, and with the breath of his lips shall he slay the wicked" (vs. 2-4).

The Branch of Jehovah apparently refers to the divine nature of this end-time Redeemer. In verses 5 through 9 of this same chapter, Isaiah prophetically reveals as well how an Edenic existence is to be ushered in, for, "...in that day there shall be a root of Jesse, which shall stand for an ensign of the people; to it shall the Gentiles seek: and his rest shall be glorious" (v. 10).

This end-time prophecy reinforces how the nations will come to an awareness of Israel's Messiah, whereas Israel will not come to this understanding until His return in power. Israel remains blind to this day, in spite of the clarity of the program that is detailed here.

Jeremiah, as does Isaiah, speaks of the Branch, the end-time Redeemer. In Jer. 23 the prophet chastises the shepherds, or spiritual leaders, of Israel who have failed in their appointed mission to guard the flock: "Behold, the days come, saith the Lord, that I will raise unto David a righteous Branch, and a King shall prosper, and shall execute judgment and justice in the earth. In his days Judah shall be saved, and Israel shall dwell safely: and this is his name whereby he shall be called, THE LORD OUR RIGHTEOUSNESS [*Jehovah Tsidkenu*]" (vs. 5-6).

As in other clearly messianic passages, He must be perfect and righteous, without the possibility of failure. How unlike God's servant David (and servant Israel) who, in Ps. 143:1-2 declares: "Hear my prayer, O Lord, give ear to my supplications: in thy faithfulness answer me, and in thy righteousness. And enter not into judgment with thy servant: for in thy sight shall no man living be justified."

God alone can claim the title *Jehovah Tsidkenu* and physically reign as King, bring universal peace and restore the harmony seen in the Garden of Eden. Since the prophecy of Isaiah chapter 11 is inarguably messianic, the parallel passages here in Jeremiah should be seen in the same light. It is increasingly difficult to ignore that Messiah, although coming in the flesh, is Divine.

In the 33rd chapter of Jeremiah, the theme of restoration and the role of the servant identified as the Branch is continued. "In those days, and at that time, will I cause the Branch of righteousness to grow up unto David; and he shall execute judgment and righteousness in the land. In those days shall Judah be saved, and Jerusalem shall dwell safely: and this is the name wherewith she shall be called, The Lord our righteousness" (vs. 15-16).

Zechariah 3:8-10 adds that the day would come when God's servant, the Branch, will remove the iniquity of the land. Continuing in chapter 6 (vs.12-13), Zechariah adds: "And speak unto him, saying, Thus speaketh the Lord of hosts, saying, Behold the man whose name is The BRANCH; and he shall grow up out of his place, and he shall build the temple of the Lord: Even he shall build the temple of the Lord; and he shall bear the glory, and shall sit and rule upon his throne; and he shall be a priest upon his throne: and the counsel of peace shall be between them both."

It has been well established that the Branch will usher in a time of equity and peace, rule in holiness and possess a Divine nature.

Now we see that He not only sits upon the throne of Judah as our King, but is to be a priest as well. Traditionally, the priestly tribe is the Levite, and Judah is the tribe of the kings. The next chapter will explain how this seeming contradiction not only is in harmony with the scriptures, but is consistent with the prediction that Messiah is, indeed, the prophet like Moses promised in Deuteronomy 18.

3

THE PROPHET LIKE MOSES

Parallels between the lives of Moses and Jesus were mentioned earlier, and included both starting in positions of power and authority, possessing great wealth, enjoying favored status, experiencing reversal of fortune, disappearing from view and reappearing later to serve a role in redemption.

Moses is not only described as a servant of God, but he is called a lawgiver and king. Per Deut. 33:4-5: "Moses commanded us a law, even the inheritance of the congregation of Jacob. And he was king in Jeshurun, when the heads of the people and the tribes of Israel were gathered together."

A priest or mediator is the intermediate between man and God. He represents the people to the Lord, and likewise talks in God's behalf to man. Moses, and Aaron his brother, were Levites, qualifying as mediators before the Lord. Moses was permitted to enter the Tabernacle and to ascend the mount of God, whereas the people were warned that they would perish if they were to come too close. As testimony to the special relationship enjoyed by Moses, it is recorded: "And the Lord spake unto Moses face to face, as a man speaketh unto his friend" (Ex. 33:11).

In Ex. 32:9 we see that God declared the nation to be stiffnecked, and said, "Now therefore let me alone, that my wrath may wax hot against them, and that I may consume them..." (v. 10). Moses proceeded to intercede on their behalf, on the basis of which, "And Jehovah repented of the evil which he said he would do unto his people" (v. 14).

Considering all this, in conjunction with the testimony that the Branch will sit upon the throne and be a priest, we can expect another parallel between Moses and the Promised One. However, there would appear to be a problem in that Messiah is from the tribe of Judah, and is not a Levite like Moses. This can be explained by examining Psalm 110.

We saw earlier that this psalm of David is quoted in supporting our discussion on the two comings. The Lord was to sit on the right hand of God until His enemies were to become His footstool. Verse 4 of the psalm adds: "The Lord hath sworn, and will not repent, Thou art a priest for ever after the order of Melchizedek." Messiah's identity as a priest does not require coming from the tribe of Levi.

First we must note that *Melchizedek* is a compound of two Hebrew words, *melech* (king), and *tzedek* (righteous). The One for Whom we look is righteous, whereas no human can be. He is not described as being of the Levitical order, but rather akin to the mysterious figure we met in Genesis, called the king of Salem (peace) and the priest of the most High God. God alone can state with certainty that we are to look for One He calls righteous, and capable of bringing in an eternal priesthood, unlike the temporary and transitional Levitical order.

There are other similarities between Jesus and Moses which render further credence to fulfilled prophecy. Both were preserved from death at the time of birth. Per Exodus 2, Moses was not put to death as was required by Pharaoh's decree, but was cast among the bulrushes where he was saved by the daughter of Pharaoh. Similarly, Herod, in seeking to destroy any potential inheritor to his throne, issued a decree to kill all those who were born in Bethlehem around the time the wise men came to inquire of the birth of the One Whose star they followed (Matthew 2).

Moses is described in Exodus 7 as battling the forces of evil in contending with the magicians of Egypt. They performed satanic miracles to mirror the signs given him by God. These sorcerers used enchantments to turn their rods into serpents and turned the water into blood, etc. Jesus had direct confrontation with Satan in the wilderness as reported in Matthew 4.

When Moses ascended the mount of God to receive the tablets, he did not eat for forty days or nights (Ex. 34:28). The account in Matthew 4 indicates that Jesus was tempted of the devil after having fasted for forty days and nights.

In escaping the advancing army of the Egyptians, Moses parted the seas so that Israel could pass over on dry ground (Exodus 14). Jesus also exercised control over the sea when He and His disciples were beset by a tempest (Matthew 8).

Both Moses and Jesus fed the multitudes in miraculous fashion. In Exodus 16, Moses brought forth quail to satisfy the craving of the people, and Jesus provided for the masses with a few fish and several loaves of bread (Matt. 14:15-21).

When Moses came down from Mount Sinai with the tablets of the law, it is written that the skin of his face shown radiantly (Exodus 34). According to Matthew 17, Jesus was transfigured before the people and "...his face did shine as the sun..." (v. 2).

It was recorded that they both withstood the murmuring of the people. One such incident is recorded in Exodus 17 when the nation complained of not having water to drink. Similarly, they found fault with Jesus in Mark 7 when they accused the disciples of eating with unwashed hands (not being ceremonially clean, according to Jewish tradition).

Numbers 12 tells us that Moses had to endure the accusations of his own brother and sister, for Aaron and Miriam spoke against him with regard to his marrying an Ethiopian. John 7 testifies of Jesus that, "For neither did his brethren believe in him" (v. 5).

As recorded in Numbers 11 and Luke 10, both Moses and Jesus had seventy helpers to assist their ministries. They each are described as having made intercessory prayer to God on behalf of the nation, and both were credited with having established memorials. Moses instituted the Passover, and Jesus the counterpart in the Last Supper, a *seder* that was to memorialize His sacrifice.

Most importantly, we point out that which is consistent with the theme of the two comings of the Messiah; for Moses and Jesus appeared before the nation subsequent to their deaths. Matthew 17 not only records the transfiguration of Jesus, but adds that Moses was also upon the mount (as was Elijah, who prophetically will herald the return of Messiah). Following the crucifixion, it is pointed out in Acts 1:3: "To whom also he shewed himself alive after his passion by many infallible proofs, being seen of them forty days, and speaking of the things pertaining to the kingdom of God..." Jesus appeared to Mary Magdalene after He arose on the first day of the week, and then appeared to two disciples as they were walking on the road to Emmaus. This was followed by His visiting the remaining eleven apostles as they sat at meat. In short, there is ample reference to see the ministry of the Messiah played out in the life of Moses, and to realize that a foundation has been laid to look for a second coming. Judaism recognizes the hope of the resurrection, and that hope is inexorably bound up in the Messiah who conquers death and hell.

Before leaving the subject of these comparisons, it is worthy of mention that the character of Moses provides insight as well in what might be expected of the promised Messiah. We find fault with a savior who is meek and gentle, because we look for the champion who destroys the enemies of the nation. However, Moses is described as being the meekest upon the face of the earth (Num. 12:3).

We know from many passages already cited that Messiah is to have the spirit of God. Another dimension to His character, consistent with the attribute of meekness ascribed to Moses, is found in Isaiah 42. "Behold my servant, whom I uphold; mine elect, in whom my soul delighteth; I have put my spirit upon him...He shall not cry, nor lift up, nor cause his voice to be heard in the street. A bruised reed shall he not break, and the smoking flax shall he not quench: he shall bring forth judgment unto truth. He shall not fail nor be discouraged, till he have set judgment in the earth: and the isles shall wait for his law" (vs. 1-4).

The unobtrusive qualities described in these first four verses do not in any way reflect the nature of Israel. The One mentioned here is to be supernaturally gentle and meek. He would not even break a slender reed that is barely hanging by a thread, nor cause the flame of a flickering candle to be extinguished as He walks by. In spite of such tenderness and humility, He would be resolute and accomplish the objectives of God in maintaining righteousness and equity.

Israel, we know, was to be *Or Lagoyim* (the light to the nations), but was inconsistent in providing that light. This Servant was not to fail. It would be normal to expect a glorious conqueror to come riding triumphantly on a majestic white steed, yet even Zechariah announces: "Rejoice greatly, O daughter of Zion; shout, O daughter of Jerusalem: behold, thy King cometh unto thee: he is just, and having salvation; lowly, and riding upon an ass, and upon a colt the foal of an ass" (9:9).

Verses 6-7 of Isaiah 42 continue to show the very special nature of this Spirit-filled Servant: "I the Lord have called thee in righteousness, and will hold thine hand, and will keep thee, and give thee for a covenant of the people, for a light of the Gentiles; To open the blind eyes, to bring out the prisoners from the prison, and them that sit in darkness out of the prison house."

This Servant is to be given as a covenant for Israel and for the nations. There is no way that unrighteous Israel could be offered or deemed acceptable as a holy offering. It would be superfluous to repeat the many Biblical references already cited; it is enough to say that it would take the blood of the Lamb of God to cover man's sin and bring both Jew and Gentile before the throne of grace.

Isaiah 42:3, in referring to the "bruised reed" and "smoking flax", is actually describing the spiritual condition of Israel at the time Messiah comes. Our Jewish brothers and sisters perceive Israel as the servant. We feel strongly, however, the Messiah is the Servant, and Israel the flickering candle, the broken reed.

Israel was called to be *Or Lagoyim*, the "light to the nations". That light was in danger of being extinguished. Having failed in their testimony, Israel was all but snuffed out and broken off. But for the grace of God, this would be their fate.

The ultimate Servant, Messiah Jesus, by contrast, is the gentle One Who would not quench the light. It is He, of Whom it is written, Who would correct Israel in measure, but not utterly destroy them (Jer. 30:11). Israel is preserved by grace to become that light, which is to testify of God's faithfulness.

In an apocalyptic *midrash, Otot ha moshiach*, (signs of the messiah), it is recorded that we will recognize the coming of the anointed one, for he will open the eyes of the blind. Not only were the physically blind to be healed, but those in spiritual darkness, those imprisoned by a sin nature and bound by tradition, would experience God's healing power.

Isaiah 42:22-24 adds: "But this is a people robbed and spoiled; they are all of them snared in holes, and they are hid in prison houses: they are for a prey, and none delivereth; for a spoil, and none saith, Restore. Who among you will give ear to this? who will hearken and hear for the time to come? Who gave Jacob for a spoil, and Israel to the robbers? did not the Lord, he against whom we have sinned? for they would not walk in his ways, neither were they obedient unto his law."

There can be no doubt that God takes the blame for Israel's fate, and reveals it to be the direct consequence of their transgressions. It is for this reason that the Servant introduced here came and set things right.

The picture we have thus far demands that the Servant and Redeemer be supernaturally righteous, uncompromising with sin, have the Spirit upon Him, be a prophet like Moses, a priest and king, exhibit meekness, come from the stem of Jesse, bear Divine titles and be manifested in the flesh.

In the opening chapter of Micah (1:2-3), the admonition is: "Hear, all ye people; hearken, O earth, and all that therein is: and let the Lord God be witness against you, the Lord from his holy temple. For, behold, the Lord cometh forth out of his place, and will come down, and tread upon the high places of the earth." Lest we take this to be poetic or symbolic, consider too: "But thou, Bethlehem Ephratah, though thou be little among the thousands of Judah, yet out of thee shall he come forth unto me that is to be ruler in Israel;

whose goings forth have been from of old, from everlasting" (5:2).

It was anticipated that Messiah would come from Judah, the city of the kings of Israel. However, this prophetic vision tells us that Messiah would come from the insignificant (the least of thousands) town of Bethlehem, David's birthplace. The One born here Who is to reign is the Promised One for Whom the nation has been waiting from time immemorial. "And he shall stand and feed in the strength of the Lord, in the majesty of the name of the Lord his God; and they shall abide: for now shall he be great unto the ends of the earth. And this man shall be the peace..." (vs. 4-5).

In Isaiah 9:2 we saw that, "The people that walked in darkness have seen a great light: they that dwell in the land of the shadow of death, upon them hath the light shined." Now in the 42nd chapter (v. 16), Isaiah adds: "And I will bring the blind by a way that they knew not...I will make darkness light before them, and crooked things straight..." In opening the spiritually blind eyes, God prepares a path so that those who rejected His Messiah would now understand and recognize the Servant.

The nation Israel was, beyond a doubt, a servant, but these passages make it clear that the supernatural power and accomplishments are indicative of the Servant par excellence, *Moshiach ben David*, the Son of David.

4

THE SUFFERING SERVANT

Isaiah 53 opens with a question: "Who hath believed our report? and to whom is the arm of the Lord revealed?" We stated earlier that the arm of the Lord is used in such a way so as to personify an individual, and express more than symbolic salvation. It is appropriate at this juncture to answer this question and reveal exactly who the arm of the Lord is.

In the 51st chapter, Isaiah calls Israel to attention: "Hearken unto me, my people; and give ear unto me, O my nation: for a law shall proceed from me, and I will make my judgment to rest for a light of the people. My righteousness is near; my salvation is gone forth, and mine arms shall judge the people; the isles shall wait upon me, and on mine arm shall they trust" (vs. 4-5). He adds in vs. 9-10: "Awake, awake, put on strength, O arm of the Lord; awake, as in the ancient days, in the generations of old. Art thou not it that hath cut Rahab, and wounded the dragon? Art thou not it which hath dried the sea, the waters of the great deep; that hath made the depths of the sea a way for the ransomed to pass over?"

Continuing to personify the "arm" in chapter 52:10, we read: "The Lord hath made bare his holy arm in the eyes of all the nations; and all the ends of the earth shall see the salvation of our God." Once more, similar terminology is used in the 63rd chapter in verse 5: "And I looked, and there was none to help; and I wondered that there was none to uphold: therefore mine own arm brought salvation unto me; and my fury, it upheld me."

Subsequent to inquiring as to whom the arm is revealed, we are informed: "For he shall grow up before him as a tender plant, and as a root out of a dry ground..." (53:2). This might initially suggest that Israel is in view, but a closer look is required. Let's backtrack for a moment to Isaiah 11:1, which was mentioned earlier. A rod was to come forth out of the stem of Jesse and a Branch out of his roots.

David is the son of Jesse and the Messiah is to come through his lineage. The Spirit of the Lord was to rest upon Him, and He was to exhibit supernatural qualities (not judging by sight or sound, being righteous, reproving with equity, smiting the earth with the rod of His mouth and slaying the wicked with the breath of His lips).

The picture before us is that of the nation of Israel seemingly vanquished, compared to a tree that has been chopped down, with only a stump remaining in the ground. Although it would seem to be dead, a sprig or shoot suddenly forms from the stump and begins to grow, bringing life from the dead. Messiah in like fashion comes when hope has been lost. Further, His being born of a virgin, like the sprig from the seemingly dead stump, is life from the dead. Since Messiah is to come from the seed of David, the nation of Israel must survive.

Verse 2 of chapter 53 describes His growing up as a root out of a dry ground. This too is a fitting description for a virgin giving birth; having an unfertilized womb is akin to bringing life where there would seem to be no source of nourishment.

Additional insight as to the identity of the One to emerge as a root out of the dry ground is obtained from a spiritual application. The children of Israel, upon exiting Egypt, traveled three days without water. Water was finally spotted, but when they drew near, their disappointment was compounded, because "...they could not drink of the waters of Marah, for they were bitter: therefore the name of it was called Marah. And the people murmured against Moses, saying, What shall we drink? And he cried unto the Lord; and the Lord shewed him a tree, which when he had cast into the waters, the waters were made sweet: there he made for them a statute and an ordinance, and there he proved [tested] them..." (Ex. 15:23-25).

God revealed to Moses that the tree out of the dry ground could turn the polluted waters sweet, drinkable, life-sustaining. We see here that Jesus is the Root out of the dry ground, and now understand that this is the lesson that was to be an ordinance for Israel. When Jesus is added to the equation, we receive life from the dead; the bitter is made sweet, and our provision is in Him. This is not readily understood, for God must open our eyes, as He did Moses'.

These observations alone do not necessarily prove that Messiah, rather than Israel, is in view, so we must continue to examine the evidence before us. A proper perspective requires that we start in the closing verses of Isaiah 52, which lead up to what we've seen thus far.

Verses 13-14 introduce, or begin to paint, a portrait for our inspection: "Behold, my servant shall deal prudently, he shall be exalted and extolled, and be very high. As many were astonied at thee; his visage was so marred more than any man, and his form more than the sons of men..."

As the canvas begins to fill in, we still have two possibilities, for neither Israel nor the Messiah can be counted out as yet. The description here is of One who will be wise, exalted and made very high. A clue to His being lifted up may be seen in the incident where Moses lifted up the serpent in the wilderness, and those who looked upon it were granted life.

In the messianic Psalm 22, Messiah refers to Himself as "...a worm, and no man; a reproach of men, and despised of the people" (v. 6). Venomous snakes or fiery serpents were sent as God's punishment to bite and slay those who murmured and complained against Him. However, those who looked up to the serpent of brass were revived.

This contrasts those who regard Messiah as a worm or snake (satanic), to those who see Him high and lifted up. Spiritual death is the end for the one who rejects Him, but he who sees Jesus lifted up is granted eternal life. Messiah is our *kohen gadol*, or high priest, ascended into heaven to make intercession and obtain eternal redemption through His blood.

In Leviticus 10:17, in referring to the sin offering, it is recorded: "...God hath given it to you to bear [elevate or lift up, or, in effect, forgive] the iniquity of the congregation, to make atonement for them before the Lord..." In shedding His blood, Messiah bore the iniquity and provided the atonement. The accomplishment of His mission exalted Him in the sight of God, and in the sight of those of us who recognize this fulfillment of prophecy.

No doubt Israel has suffered greatly as a nation, and could well be described as having been scarred or disfigured. Messiah, too, is to suffer, and historically this is a most fitting description of the treatment received by Jesus. It brings into view His scourging, trial and crucifixion.

Psalm 22 describes the pain and torture: the bones out of joint and the tongue clinging to the roof of the mouth. It tells of the pierced hands and feet, the heart melting in the midst of His bowels and the torn flesh. This mutilation aptly conforms to the description of one whose visage or appearance is marred more than any man, and causes astonishment.

Continuing in Is. 52:15: "So shall he sprinkle many nations; the kings shall shut their mouths at him: for that which had not been told them shall they see; and that which they had not heard shall they consider." In order to elicit sense from *cain yazeh goyim rabim*, "he shall sprinkle many nations", we must look to the Hebrew language for help. The root of the word *yazeh* is *nazah*, to sprinkle, especially in expiation. This is the clear application seen in Num. 8:7, Lev. 14:7 and Ex. 29:21, all of which speak of sprinkling the water of purification, sprinkling blood to cleanse a leper, and the blood of a ram to hallow Aaron and his sons. Messiah is to sprinkle or cover us with His blood.

It is also mentioned in verse 15 that "...kings shall shut their mouths at him...that which they had not heard shall they consider." Many Gentile nations of the past were not told of Israel's Messiah. When Jesus returns, they will see what they had not been told, for they will behold Jesus ascending to the throne of Israel.

We have already discussed Israel's sin which invalidates the nation from imputing righteousness to another, but we note that some will argue that Israel is still in view in this passage. The language used here in Isaiah closely resembles that which is expressed in Micah

7:16: "The nations shall see and be confounded at all their might: they shall lay their hand upon their mouth, their ears shall be deaf." We have never denied that many parallels exist between the servant, Israel, and the ultimate Servant, Messiah. In separating the two it is essential to distinguish that which accurately depicts the Sinless One, and the nation that failed to match the perfection demanded by Levitical law.

Micah, therefore, adds in verses 18-20: "Who is a God like unto thee, that pardoneth iniquity, and passeth by the transgression of the remnant of his heritage? he retaineth not his anger for ever, because he delighteth in mercy. He will turn again, he will have compassion upon us; he will subdue our iniquities; and thou wilt cast all their sins into the depths of the sea. Thou wilt perform the truth to Jacob, and mercy to Abraham, which thou hast sworn unto our fathers from the days of old."

This clearly is a picture of a nation that failed and requires the justification of a merciful God Who keeps His covenant promises. The Servant of Is. 52-53, on the other hand, is depicted as an innocent sufferer Who stops not only the mouths of the nations, but unregenerate Israel who now will consider what they were told, but denied heretofore.

Back in Isaiah 41 the Lord addresses Israel: "But thou, Israel, art my servant, Jacob whom I have chosen, the seed of Abraham my friend. Thou whom I have taken from the ends of the earth, and called thee from the chief men thereof, and said unto thee, Thou art my servant; I have chosen thee, and not cast thee away" (vs. 8-9).

In contrast to the sinless Servant, Israel will not be cast away, but must depend upon God's mercy for deliverance. Thus Is. 41:10-11 continues: "Fear thou not; for I am with thee: be not dismayed; for I am thy God: I will strengthen thee; yea, I will help thee; yea, I will uphold thee with the right hand of my righteousness. Behold, all they that were incensed against thee shall be ashamed and confounded: they shall be as nothing; and they that strive with thee shall perish."

In greater emphasis, verse 14 adds: "Fear not, thou worm Jacob, and ye men of Israel; I will help thee, saith the Lord, and thy redeemer, the Holy One of Israel." How much clearer can it be? Israel needs redemption, and is it not the Holy One Who achieves this goal?

Chapter 41 concludes: "For I beheld, and there was no man; even among them, and there was no counsellor, that, when I asked of them, could answer a word. Behold, they are all vanity; their works are nothing: their molten images are wind and confusion" (vs. 28-29). The inadequacy of Israel is then contrasted with the ultimate Servant introduced in chapter 42. He is the Elect, the Spirit-filled, gentle Redeemer who brings justice to both Jew and Gentile.

Isaiah continues to develop the theme and to describe the person and work of the Servant Who will accomplish God's purpose. His description in chapter 52 melds with David's portrait in Psalm 2. Here we were told that: "The kings of the earth set themselves, and the rulers take counsel together, against the Lord, and against his anointed, saying, Let us break their bands asunder, and cast away their cords from us" (vs. 2-3).

The heathen rages and the kings defy the Lord, but per vs. 4-12: "He that sitteth in heavens shall laugh: the Lord shall have them in derision. Then shall he speak unto them in his wrath, and vex them in his sore displeasure. Yet have I set my king upon my holy hill of Zion. I will declare the decree: the Lord hath said unto me, Thou art my Son; this day have I begotten thee. Ask of me, and I shall give thee the heathen for thine inheritance, and the uttermost parts of the earth for thy possession. Thou shalt break them with a rod of iron: thou shalt dash them in pieces like a potter's vessel. Be wise now therefore, O ye kings: be instructed, ye judges of the earth. Serve the Lord with fear, and rejoice with trembling. Kiss the Son, lest he be angry, and ye perish from the way, when his wrath is kindled but a little. Blessed are all they that put their trust in him."

Clearly the time is to come when mouths will be stopped in astonishment, and the nations will realize and see the power of God's Anointed. Once again, the nations have indeed made a prey of Israel, but these passages speak of the Lord God and His Messiah, against Whom they rage and before Whom they ultimately will be brought into subjection. At that point they will do homage (kiss the son) and bend the knee to the One who sits upon Zion's throne.

In chapter 53:1, Isaiah asks the question, "...to whom is the arm of the Lord revealed?" We not only see the "arm" as a person, Jesus, but have commented on how this thought is preceded with the statement: "...he shall grow up...as a tender plant..." (v. 2). Although the Hebrew *ca-yonek* is translated as "tender plant" or "small shoot", the more appropriate terminology is "a suckling child".

Deut. 32:25 indicates that the sword shall destroy without, and there will be terror within, for "...both the young man and the virgin, the suckling (*yonek*) also with the man of gray hairs." This reference to the infant links Messiah to the prophecy of Is. 7:14 and 9:6, the Savior born into the world. Certainly we can say, "Who has believed our report?", for most seek the hero-and-warrior redeemer, not the Child who is "Immanuel", God with us.

It is interesting to note as well that Messiah, the prophet like Moses, came into the world inconspicuously as did Moses, but was to grow up and ultimately be revealed as the Redeemer.

Verse 2 of Isaiah 53 adds, "...he hath no form nor comeliness...", for He did not fit the preconceived image of the One for Whom Israel looked, the king on the white charger. Just as Messiah was to be born in the insignificant town of Bethlehem, and not Judah, and as He was to be meek and lowly, riding upon an ass, He remains consistent to the prophecy in having no attraction, and exercising no power or authority.

Beyond this, His reception would not mirror the expectation of the people. For a limited time Jesus had the support of the commoners, but ultimately He would be spat upon, ridiculed, crowned with thorns, nailed to a tree and left alone. It was expedient that He be the scapegoat rather than permit His doctrine to threaten traditional concepts and bring disfavor from the Roman rulers of Judea.

Not only does the Servant described by Isaiah fail to meet our expectations, having no comeliness or appeal; verse 3 continues: "He is despised and rejected of men; a man of sorrows [pains], and acquainted with grief [disease]: and we hid as it were our faces from him; he was despised, and we esteemed him not."

Earlier, in 49:1, Isaiah wrote of the servant called from the womb. Verse 5 states that He would be formed "...from the womb to be his [God's] servant..."; that His role would be "...to bring Jacob again to him, though Israel be not gathered...", and that He would "...be glorious in the eyes of the Lord..."

Per verse 6, He was to be "...my servant to raise up the tribes of Jacob, and to restore the preserved of Israel..."; to be "...for a light to the Gentiles...", and be "...my salvation to the ends of the earth." The contrast is obvious: called and blessed by God, but despised and rejected by men. In fact, "Thus saith the Lord, the Redeemer of Israel, and his Holy One, to him whom man despiseth, to him whom the nation abhorreth, to a servant of rulers, Kings shall see and arise, princes also shall worship, because of the Lord that is faithful, and the Holy One of Israel, and he shall choose thee" (49:7).

As seen in Isaiah 52, the time will come when the astonished mouths will be stopped, but first this Servant is to be held in contempt by kings, by the nations and by His own people. We interject that the subject of this chapter is referred to as a 'servant of rulers". This, too, is significant, because the One who would be a king in His own right, for now submits to all authority. This is the picture of Jesus, Who did not defy the power of Rome, and waits for the time to return as Lord of lords, as King of kings.

Thus Isaiah continues (53:4): "Surely he hath borne our griefs, and carried our sorrows: yet we did esteem him stricken, smitten of God, and afflicted." The Servant of Jehovah is stricken and smitten by God; He suffers anguish and humiliation, both physical and emotional torment. While it may be said that Israel fits this description, the role here is of One who endures the ignominious treatment on another's behalf. He bore "our" sorrows and griefs. Is this Israel?

All the prophets told of God's blessings for obedience, and

constantly warned of the consequences of disobedience. Moses told the nation: "And it shall come to pass, if thou shalt hearken diligently unto the voice of the Lord thy God, to observe and to do all his commandments which I command thee this day, that the Lord thy God will set thee on high above all nations of the earth: And all these blessings shall come on thee, and overtake thee...And the Lord shall make thee plenteous in goods, in the fruit of thy body, and in the fruit of thy cattle, and in the fruit of thy ground, in the land which the Lord sware unto thy fathers to give thee...But it shall come to pass, if thou wilt not hearken unto the voice of the Lord thy God, to observe to do all his commandments and his statutes which I command thee this day; that all these curses shall come upon thee, and overtake thee...The Lord shall send upon thee cursing, vexation, and rebuke, in all that thou settest thine hand unto for to do, until thou be destroyed...The Lord shall make the pestilence cleave unto thee...The Lord shall smite thee with a consumption, and with a fever, and with an inflammation, and with an extreme burning...The Lord shall cause thee to be smitten before thine enemies...The Lord will smite thee with the botch of Egypt...Thy sons and thy daughters shall be given unto another people..." (Deut. 28:1-2, 11, 15, 20-22, 25, 27, 32).

A cause-and-effect relationship is clearly established. Faithfulness is to be blessed, while disobedience demands punishment. A holy God Who cannot lie would not punish Israel for being a proper testimony. Rather, Israel has always suffered as a direct consequence of their obstinacy. As a father punishes a wayward child, the Lord chastised Israel for their correction, but not to their destruction.

The psalmist confesses (Ps. 118:17-18): "I shall not die, but live, and declare the works of the Lord. The Lord hath chastened me sore: but he hath not given me over unto death." Unlike the servant, Israel, punished by a righteous God Who does not indulge sin, the Servant of Isaiah 52 and 53 is One who "...had done no violence, neither was any deceit in his mouth"; and "...by his knowledge shall my righteous servant justify many; for he shall bear their iniquities" (Is. 53:9, 11).

If Israel were righteous and without deceit, God would be unfaithful and deceitful in doling out this punishment. If Israel is guilty, and justly punished, they would not qualify as the vicarious, innocent substitute required by Levitical law. A proper conclusion is that the spotless Lamb of God, Israel's Messiah, is depicted here as the appropriate offering.

Commentaries, including that of Yochanan ben Uzziel's *targum* of Isaiah, wrote that Jehovah's Servant would suffer vicariously for Israel, and that the nation would be forgiven for His sake. Other rabbinical works reveal the same understanding: God asked Messiah to bear the afflictions of His people to be their atonement. Messiah is referred to as *ha naguah*, the leprous one, for He would bear our diseases, and so reconcile us to God.

We spoke before of how Messiah's being lifted up does not simply predict His ultimate recognition and acceptance, but the mediatorial role of the priest in expiation. In like manner, the Hebrew *nasah* for "borne" and "carried" are used in the book of Leviticus in discussing the atonement provided (or borne) by sacrifice. Sinful Israel could never be that acceptable atonement upon God's holy altar. Israel never willingly suffered, but the servant here voluntarily accepts this role to satisfy the requirements of a holy law and holy God.

It is argued that the righteous remnant of Israel bears this burden, but historically we see no evidence, and Biblically we see this as a contradiction. The heart of man has never changed, and the Lord would be as hard-pressed in every generation to find even the ten righteous unavailable to circumvent the destruction of Sodom. We are reminded in Psalm 49:7 that, "None of them can by any means redeem his brother, nor give to God a ransom [atonement] for him..."

Our portrait is further enhanced in Is. 53:5 in the declaration: "But he was wounded for our transgressions, he was bruised for our iniquities: the chastisement of our peace was upon him; and with his stripes we are healed." In pointing to the vicarious, horrendous nature of the pain inflicted upon the Servant, the Hebrew word translated as "wounded" is *chalal*, which means "to bore" or "pierce".

It is no accident that Psalm 22, which describes the crucifixion, likewise tells us that they pierced His hands and His feet. The Hebrew scriptures present it: "...Like lions, they threaten my hands and my feet..." (v. 17MT), which suggests to some that, as a lion's bite pierces the skin, so the Servant is put in jeopardy. In an even more obvious parallel, some scholars insist that *caw-ari* does not actually refer to a lion, for the vowels, which are the basis for this rendering, were added later, and misrepresent the true intent. The more accurate definition is to bore through, or pierce.

In Ps. 40:6 the same root word is used, and the Hebrew translates the thought as, "...mine ears hast thou opened...", or "hollowed out". Drawing from Levitical law, when a slave served his term of indenture, but chose not to be set free because he opted to remain with his master, he would have his ear bored through with an awl. This was a sign of his continual service and commitment. Jehovah's Servant thus testifies that His ear has been bored or pierced as the evidence of total submission to God.

Ironically, Jewish critics have told me that Psalm 40 proves that God does not want or deem sacrifices as essential. Verse 6 declares: "Sacrifice and offering thou didst not desire; mine ears hast thou opened: burnt offering and sin offering hast thou not required." Since we know God does not contradict Himself, we are meant to understand that commitment and a right attitude are to be preferred above ritual.

In the first chapter of Isaiah, God asserts that He takes no delight in sacrifices or in the blood of bulls and lambs. He continues (v. 13): "Bring no more vain oblations; incense is an abomination unto me; the new moons and sabbaths, the calling of assemblies, I cannot away with; it is iniquity, even the solemn meeting." All the ritual and performing of *mitzvahs* (good deeds) is of no consequence if your heart is not right with God.

Clarification follows by means of the explanation: "Learn to do well; seek judgment, relieve the oppressed, judge the fatherless, plead for the widow" (v. 17). Psalm 40 then bears out that the Lord's Servant, like a slave choosing to remain with his master, accepts and desires the opportunity to surrender completely. Isaiah uses language to show that the Servant is not merely wounded, but pierced for this purpose.

The willingness of this Servant will bear fruit when, according to Zechariah 12 we will "...look upon me whom they have pierced, and they shall mourn for him, as one mourneth for his only son, and shall be in bitterness for him, as one that is in bitterness for his firstborn."

Beyond the piercing of the Servant, Isaiah states that He is "bruised" which is rendered from the Hebrew *da-cah*. This word carries the meaning "to crush" or "grind to powder". This is the term used in Genesis in referring to Messiah's victory over Satan, when He shall bruise or crush his head in delivering the death blow.

A most horrible and painful death is depicted to evoke our understanding of the role played by this Servant. He is the willing recipient of this torture, so that "...the chastisement of our peace..." (Is. 53:5) would be upon Him. Achieving peace with God for us cost Him dearly, and this was not a price that Israel could pay. Thus the verse concludes "...with his stripes we are healed." But the use of the Hebrew, *chaver*, which is translated as "stripes", tells us much more.

Chaver is also the word for "friend", and in Is. 1:23 is translated as "companion". Consider God's message: our identification with Messiah is the means through which we are spiritually healed and have peace with God. He took upon Himself the penalty of sin so that we might have His imputed righteousness in exchange.

The attitude of the world is clear from Is. 53: 6: "All we like sheep have gone astray; we have turned everyone to his own way; and the Lord hath laid on him the iniquity of us all." Attributing these verses to righteous Israel is again contradicted, since "we all" have gone astray and He bears the iniquity of "us all".

Psalm 22:23 concurs, for the confession is: "Ye that fear the Lord, praise him; all ye the seed of Jacob, glorify him; and fear him, all ye the seed of Israel." So all are guilty, and all must confess and bow the knee. Israel in its entirety was pronounced guilty, and Messiah had to accomplish what Israel failed to do.

Further indication as to the identity of this Servant is revealed in the reference to the sheep having gone astray. Sheep require a shepherd, and the spiritual leaders of Israel were meant to guide the flock of God. Ezekiel makes it obvious that this is one more area where the people of God had failed.

"And the word of the Lord came unto me, saying, Son of man, prophesy against the shepherds of Israel, prophesy, and say unto them, Thus saith the Lord God unto the shepherds; Woe be to the shepherds of Israel that do feed themselves! should not the shepherds feed the flocks? Ye eat the fat, and ye clothe you with the wool, ye kill them that are fed: but ye feed not the flock. The diseased have ye not strengthened, neither have ye healed that which was sick, neither have ye bound up that which was broken, neither have ye brought again that which was driven away, neither have ye sought that which was lost; but with force and with cruelty have ye ruled them. And they were scattered, because there is no shepherd: and they became meat to all the beasts of the field, when they were scattered" (Ezek. 34:1-5).

Judgment is pronounced upon the spiritual leaders in verses 9-10: "Therefore, O ye shepherds, hear the word of the Lord; Thus saith the Lord God; Behold, I am against the shepherds; and I will require my flock at their hand, and cause them to cease from feeding the flock; neither shall the shepherds feed themselves any more; for I will deliver my flock from their mouth, that they may not be meat for them."

Not only does the Lord hold the leaders of Israel accountable in their failure, but He must now make provision to fulfill His purpose. This is done in verses 11-12: "For thus saith the Lord God; Behold, I, even I, will both search my sheep, and seek them out. As a shepherd seeketh out his flock in the day that he is among his sheep that are scattered; so will I seek out my sheep, and will deliver them out of all places where they have been scattered in the cloudy and dark day."

The identity of this Shepherd is then made clear (vs. 23-24): "And I will set up one shepherd over them, and he shall feed them, even my servant David; he shall feed them, and he shall be their shepherd. And I the Lord will be their God, and my servant David a prince among them; I the Lord have spoken it." The shepherds and the sheep have gone astray, but it is the Good Shepherd, Jesus, *Moshiach ben David*, who lays down His life for the sheep. As such, per verse 6 of Isaiah 53, "...the Lord hath laid on him the iniquity of us all."

Essential to our distinguishing this Servant from Israel is verse 7: "He was oppressed, and he was afflicted, yet he opened not his mouth: he is brought as a lamb to the slaughter, and as a sheep before her shearers is dumb, so he openeth not his mouth." Unlike Israel, a nation with a history of murmuring and complaining, the Servant willingly and silently suffers. This is not limited to the physical torture, but the indignities heaped upon Him by the scoffers and blasphemers.

In the second Psalm we saw the heathen raging against the Anointed One; in the 22nd Psalm, verses 7-8, it was prophesied that, "All they that see me laugh me to scorn: they shoot out the lip, they shake the head, saying, He trusted on the Lord that he would deliver him: let him deliver him, seeing he delighted in him." They taunted Jesus as He hung on the tree, deeming it absurd that God was concerned with His being delivered from this cruel fate. Yet He suffered in silence, tacitly reminding us of Ps. 40:7-8: "Then said I, Lo, I come: in the volume of the book it is written of me, I delight to do thy will, O my God: yea, thy law is within my heart."

The words uttered upon the tree by Jesus, "It is finished", spoke more eloquently than any words of protest. By His silence He acquiesced to the will of God, and distinguished Himself from the protesting nation. He was correctly identified as the Lamb of God who took away the sin of the world, and He, like a lamb, was led to the slaughter.

We saw in Is. 49:5 that the Servant was formed in the womb and named in the bowels of His mother, and was designated to raise up the tribes of Jacob, and fated to restore the preserved of Israel. He was to be the light to the nations, and yet, despised by men and abhorred by the nation. God distinguishes between the nations of the world (*goyim*) and the nation (*goy*), Israel. By using the singular form here, it reconfirms that Israel rejects the suffering servant, and can't be the subject of these verses.

According to Is. 63:7-11: "I will mention the lovingkindnesses of the Lord, and the praises of the Lord, according to all that the Lord hath bestowed on us, and the great goodness toward the house of Israel, which he hath bestowed on them according to his mercies, and according to the multitude of his lovingkindnesses. For he said, Surely they are my people, children that will not lie: so he was their Saviour. In all their affliction he was afflicted, and the angel of his presence saved them: in his love and in his pity he redeemed them; and he bare them, and carried them all the days of old. But they rebelled, and vexed his holy Spirit: therefore he was turned to be their enemy, and he fought against them. Then he remembered the days of old, Moses, and his people, saying, Where is he that brought them out of the sea with the shepherd of his flock? where is he that put his holy Spirit within him?"

What an accurate rendition of the contrasted servants! Israel, chosen to be a servant, but rebellious. Loved and pitied, in spite of constant apostasy, Israel is borne by the High Priest, the loving Shepherd, the Angel of God's *punim* (face or presence). Our Redeemer is Messiah, Who silently bears the iniquity of Israel in His love and His pity.

With the outpouring of the spirit of grace and supplication (per Zech. 12:10) comes the confession. Gazing upon Him who was pierced, Israel will ultimately see how they rebelled against God, turned their backs upon Messiah (the Angel of His presence) and vexed his Holy Spirit - all three persons of the triune God.

Jewish expositors claim these verses speak of a great general who will be slain in battle, causing devastation and bitter mourning. There is no evidence to support such a stretch of truth, nor is such an explanation consistent with this passage. Conversely, the great Talmudical rabbi, Rashi, mentions that these verses speak of Messiah ben Joseph.

Verse 8 of Isaiah 53 prophetically reveals the demise of Jehovah's servant: "He was taken from prison and from judgment: and who shall declare his generation? for he was cut off out of the land of the living: for the transgression of my people was he stricken." The scene that unfolds is that of one being judged in an oppressive manner and then being delivered for execution without objection by his generation or contemporaries. His fate was to suffer for those identified as God's people, to whom the punishment was due.

The "people" of the prophet, the "people" of God, *ammi*, is always Israel; never the *goyim*, or nations. God's Word is quite clear on this subject: "You only have I known of all the families of the earth..." (Amos 3:2).

Some argue that to be "cut off" is to be separated from Israel, and this describes the unrighteous being ostracized from the congregation. Such a conclusion is not consistent with the language, nor is it appropriate in light of Is. 53:9: "And he made his grave with the wicked, and with the rich in his death; because he had done no violence, neither was any deceit in his mouth." Daniel 9:26 (which expounds on the timetable for Messiah's appearance) avers: "And after threescore and two weeks shall Messiah be cut off, but not for himself..." We not only have confirmation of the death of Messiah, but vivid detail as to the circumstances (described in Psalm 22), and now the disposal of His body.

A criminal dying in disgrace is assigned a "...grave with the wicked...", and is not interred with his family. This, indeed, was the plan for the Crucified One. However, a rich man, Joseph of Arimathea (a town also known as Ramah, 5 miles north of Jerusalem), took Jesus' body and laid Him in his own tomb. In granting Joseph's request for the body, Pontius Pilate had no idea that he was fulfilling prophesy.

Whereas it was the norm to stone a sinner under Jewish law, Jesus was delivered up to the Romans, tried under Roman law, and executed by crucifixion. Here, too, had He been stoned, he could not have been the required Levitical sacrifice, with no bone broken. The legs of the two thieves on Jesus' right and left were broken, but Jesus being dead, they simply pierced His side with a spear. Not a bone was crushed, and it could now be stated that they looked upon Him Whom they had pierced. Is. 53:9 reminds us as well that this Servant did no violence and was not deceitful; He was innocent of the contrived charges. Pilate stated that he found no fault in Him, and would have released Him, but again, God's plan for the redemption of humanity through the blood atonement was not to be thwarted. That is why we see in verse 10: "Yet it pleased the Lord to bruise him; he hath put him to grief: when thou shalt make his soul an offering for sin, he shall see his seed, he shall prolong his days, and the pleasure of the Lord shall prosper in his hand."

It is clear from the Word that God delights in mercy and does not take delight in the death of a sinner. Per Ezek. 18:32: "For I have no pleasure in the death of him that dieth, saith the Lord God: wherefore turn yourselves, and live ye." Nevertheless, in seeming contradiction, we are told that it pleased God to bruise His righteous Servant, and takes responsibility for causing the anguish and pain. Israel was told to turn from sin and live, but Messiah's vicarious death was part of the Lord's eternal plan.

The seed of the woman (virgin) was to be bruised; the Servant of Psalm 22 would be laughed to scorn and crucified, and this was God's plan from the foundation of the world. Even the disciples who sought to protect Jesus as He moved toward His destiny were advised, "...for this cause came I into the world..." (John 18:37). Our Lord was pleased that the obedience of His Servant would satisfy the law and provide atonement for His creation.

We now realize that His soul and life force is our *kipporah*, or "covering". Man was cast out of the Garden of Eden and deprived of access to *aitz chai*, "the tree of life". The blood of Jesus provided atonement, and access was re-established. The tree of life was that which Messiah Jesus ascended at Calvary to bear or carry our sin. What an exchange! He bore our sins in His body on the tree, and we were imputed His righteousness.

In providing the atonement, Jesus would see His seed and prolong His days. Israel, now justified according to the law, by the substitutionary offering, is His seed. After the death of Messiah described in the 22nd Psalm, vs. 30-31 reveals: "A seed shall serve him; it shall be accounted to the Lord for a generation. They shall come, and shall declare his righteousness unto a people that shall be born, that he hath done this."

It is incontrovertible that Messiah had to pay the price, to suffer and die. Let us not forget, however, the expectation of Isaiah was that death would be swallowed up in victory. We will yet see the reality of Is. 45:22-25: "Look unto me, and be ye saved, all the ends of the earth: for I am God, and there is none else. I have sworn by myself, the word is gone out of my mouth in righteousness, and shall not return, That unto me every knee shall bow, every tongue shall swear. Surely, shall one say, in the Lord have I righteousness and strength: even to him shall men come; and all that are incensed against him shall be ashamed. In the Lord shall all the seed of Israel be justified, and shall glory."

We were ashamed of the One nailed to the tree, but the hostility will cease, the knee shall bow; the seed of Israel will be justified in His righteousness, and the Lord will then be pleased. Thus, it will come to pass that (Is. 53:11): "He shall see of the travail of his soul, and shall be satisfied: by his knowledge shall my righteous servant justify many; for he shall bear their iniquities."

The price was dear, but Messiah will be gratified by being obedient to God and accomplishing His purpose: justifying many, conquering sin and death and restoring the Edenic existence. The new covenant relationship of which Jeremiah 31:34 spoke will then be evident: "And they shall teach no more every man his neighbour, and every man his brother, saying, Know the Lord: for they shall all know me, from the least of them unto the greatest of them, saith the Lord: for I will forgive their iniquity, and I will remember their sin no more." The old covenant, the law engraved in stone, would be replaced by a new covenant, a new heart and new spirit; an internalization of truth. It will no longer be necessary to teach what God will put into the heart; this is the knowledge of God, the knowledge of the salvation we have in Jesus.

It is expedient at this point to go slightly off on a tangent, but this trip is well worth the time. God called Abram to come out from among them and be separate. Abram not only became Abraham, the "father of the nations", but he was the first Hebrew, from *ovair*, "to cross over" or "to be in opposition". He not only crossed over physically, but spiritually, to become the first of a nation separated unto God.

The blessing promised to Abraham for his obedience was passed to Isaac and then to Jacob. Jacob's name was changed to Israel, and his twelve sons, the tribes (or children) of Israel. His son, Judah, was the recipient of the blessing, and opened the way for his descendants to be known as Jews.

Our pride in this heritage, unfortunately, has become an obstacle. Perhaps there are those of you who experienced, as I did, a love for Jewish tradition, and a resentment toward the Gentile with whom we associate anti-semitism. Such animosity is unscriptural, for we are told to be kind to the stranger (non-Jew), for we were strangers in the land of Egypt. In any event, we were privy to the covenant of the law which brought us into a relationship with God.

Jeremiah (31:31) came with a message of a new covenant, not the covenant given when we left Egypt (the Law), but that which would be evidenced by a new heart and a new spirit through which we would know the Lord. It makes so much sense, therefore, for

Isaiah speaking in the power of the Holy Spirit: "For Zion's sake will I not hold my peace, and for Jerusalem's sake I will not rest, until the righteousness thereof go forth as brightness, and the salvation thereof as a lamp that burneth. And the Gentiles shall see thy righteousness, and all kings thy glory: and thou shalt be called by a new name, which the mouth of the Lord shall name" (Is. 62:1-2).

Since God distinguishes between Jew and Gentile only, this new name applies to the people of Zion who have new hearts and spirits; members of the new covenant nation. The Jewish people who followed Jesus were called by this new name - Christians (*Christos* is the Greek equivalent of the Hebrew, *Messiah*). Ironically, the world, and Judaism in particular, views Christianity as non-Jewish, but they fail to understand that a Christian, by definition, is a follower of Israel's Messiah, be he Gentile or a reborn Jew.

Finally, verse 12 of Isaiah 53 declares: "Therefore will I divide him a portion with the great, and he shall divide the spoil with the strong; because he hath poured out his soul unto death: and he was numbered with the transgressors; and he bare the sin of many, and made intercession for the transgressors." We have an expression today: "To the victor belongs the spoils." Having triumphed, or accomplished the will of God, the Suffering Servant is to reap the reward; God will grant Him a portion with the great.

He had been despised and they raged against Him; now He will be given honor, glory and power. At this juncture every knee will bow and every tongue confess that Jesus is Lord, to the glory of God the Father. According to Psalm 110, the people will be willing in the day of his power; all nations will worship him.

Messiah will divide the spoil with the strong; those who identified with Him and suffered for righteousness' sake. The spiritually heroic who looked for eternal, and not temporal, rewards, will now share in the glory. They will hear, "Well done, thou good and faithful servant" (Matt. 25:21).

The reason for this occurring is not to be overlooked: "...because he hath poured out his soul unto death..." (Is. 53:12). He abandoned everything, gave Himself completely, and honored the will of God. Having manifested Himself in the flesh, taking on the form of a servant, and being obedient unto death, the Servant was the epitome of humility. He took upon Himself the sins of humanity, but now is lifted up high. Proverbs 22:4 will bear out: "By humility and the fear of the Lord are riches, and honour, and life."

By bearing our sins He made intercession for us. We became the righteousness of God in Him, and now He receives the eternal glory and praise that is due. Those who were not ashamed of Him will share that reward. Here, too, it is written (Ps. 22:26-27): "The meek shall eat and be satisfied: they shall praise the Lord that seek him: your heart shall live for ever...all the kindreds of the nations shall worship before thee."

Zechariah draws a similar picture which strengthens the conclusion that this Servant is Messiah, and not Israel. "Awake, O sword, against my shepherd, and against the man that is my fellow, saith the Lord of hosts: smite the shepherd, and the sheep shall be scattered: and I will turn mine hand upon the little ones" (13:7)..."And I will bring the third part through the fire, and will refine them as silver is refined, and will try them as gold is tried...they shall say, The Lord is my God" (v. 9).

God addresses the sword (in effect, those who wield the sword), and commands the shepherd to be smitten. We have already seen that the shepherd is His Servant, the Messiah. It is He Who is smitten and killed, not Israel. This Shepherd is now called God's "fellow". Other translations render this, "against the man whom I have associated with me." The Hebrew, *ammi-ti*, clearly speaks of an equal, one of His own, so the smitten Shepherd is the One we know as Immanuel, or "God with us", the One born of the virgin.

Before leaving the subject of the Servant, we pause briefly to return to the point made in Is. 53:11, which declares: "...by his knowledge shall my righteous servant justify many; for he shall bear their iniquities." There can be no doubt that the servant is righteous, and it is his righteousness that is to be imputed to many. Unrighteous

Israel requires justification which is not of their own merit.

Interesting to note, the Hebrew Publishing Company offers a Masoretic text translated by Alexander Harkavy. He offers the following: "By his knowledge shall my servant justify the righteous before many." This puts a different slant on the passage which is more in keeping with the concept that the righteous remnant of Israel is the vicarious sufferer.

However, why would the righteous need justification? If Israel were guiltless in the sight of God, they would not need the imputed righteousness of which the prophet speaks. It is only the Servant who justifies those who are not acceptable in their own right.

Harkavy states in the preface of this translation: "The English translation accompanying the Hebrew text is the Authorized Version, known otherwise as King James Bible. The publishers have deemed this version a fit companion to the original text because its language is regarded as classic English and because it is held in great esteem throughout the English-speaking world."

He adds, however: "It has been revised and a considerable number of emendations have been made. Among the passages emended are all those which have been mistranslated or colored to suit Christian dogma."

The original stated purpose was to make the translation conformable with the rational meaning of the text, and in so doing, the "revisor has followed the best ancient and modern commentators and translators." Yet, we can see that the language is inconsistent with the King James and even with Isaac Leeser, also published by the Hebrew Publishing Company.

The Hebrew states: *B'dahto yatz-dik tzadik av-di l'ra-bim*; the singular form, *tzadik*, or "righteous one", modifies or describes *avdi*, "my servant". Thus, the King James and Leeser renditions agree it is the righteous Servant who justifies *rabim*, "many".

In his stated purpose to avoid the christological implications, Harkavy finds it more convenient to change the intent of God's prophetic vision. Christianity is oft accused of changing text to suit their opinions, but it would seem that Judaism is no stranger to serving an agenda. However sincere the mindset, it becomes obvious that we all have our inherent prejudices and preconceived ideas.

One other example comes to mind, because I spent many sessions arguing this point with a dear person who insisted the Orthodox view was intentionally destroyed by the Gentile, or King James, Bible. This involves the expression found in Psalm 2: *nishku bar*, which is translated as "kiss the son", or "do homage to the son".

There is no doubt that the Hebrew *bar* can be translated as "pure" or "holy", so, as with anything else, the context of the passage must bring enlightenment. Obviously, not all Orthodox Jews disagree with King James, for even Leeser sees this as doing homage to the son. Other passages in the scriptures bear out as well that *bar* is used for "son". Thus, attempting to remove the concept of the Son receiving the respect of the nations is moot. This is especially true when considering that the subject of the psalm, who is to mount Zion's throne, is told: "...Thou art my Son; this day have I begotten thee" (Ps. 2:7).

5

THE PLURALITY OF GOD

One of the biggest obstacles in reconciling faith in Jesus to monotheism, as understood by traditional Judaism, is, does Christianity teach a concept of three Gods? Viewing Jesus as God, the Son of God, or part of the Godhead would appear to be a total contradiction to Judaism's great profession of faith known as the *Sh'ma*. This is taken from Deut. 6:4: "Hear, O Israel, the Lord our God, the Lord is one." What can be clearer than this?

For centuries adherents to Judaism have been making this profession; our daily prayers being a constant reminder that, whereas paganism taught polytheism, a plethora of gods, Jews believe in only One: the God of Abraham, Isaac and Jacob, the God of Israel. The law given to Moses on Sinai did not simply declare this distinction, but Israel was told to bind this law upon their hearts. It was to be as frontlets before their eyes and placed upon the doorposts of their homes (Deut. 6:9).

In a most literal interpretation of the commandment, Jews to this day don *t'phillin*, or phylacteries, before reciting the morning prayers. A small box, in which is a parchment scroll containing Ex. 13:1-16, Deut. 6:4-9 and Deut. 11:13-21, is wound around the left arm (leading towards the heart), with leather straps, and a second is placed upon the forehead, as frontlets for the eyes.

The leather straps (*retzuot*), used to bind the *t'phillin* to the arm and head, as well as the parchment upon which the scriptures are written, are made from *kosher* animals and handwritten by a scribe. Males over the age of thirteen (following *bar mitzvah*) put on *t'phillin* each weekday morning, but not on the Sabbath or festivals. Inasmuch as Shabbas and holy days are in themselves reminders of the Covenant, the laying of *t'phillin* would be superfluous.

Mezuzot (literally, "doorposts") are oblong containers (usually constructed of wood, metal or plastic), some of which can be very ornate. They house the same sections of the law, and are placed on the doorpost of the entrance to the home, and in most Jewish homes, upon all the doorposts of entrances (with the exception of the bathroom). In deference to the holiness of the law, many Jewish people touch the *mezuzah* upon entering and leaving, and kiss their fingers in homage as they pass through.

Any member of the household who has reached the age of *bar* or *bas mitzvah*, and is thus old enough to understand the significance, may wear a *mezuzah* around their neck. According to the Jewish sage, Maimonides, the *mezuzah* was not to be worn as an amulet or lucky charm which would violate the *mitzvah* (commandment) and destroy the concept involving the Oneness of God and the enjoinder to love and worship Him.

Considering the positive reinforcement and constant reminder of belief in One God, Who calls Himself a jealous God, it is understandable that Judaism balks at the concept of a trinity. Many Jews have been tortured and slain for refusing to profane or renounce their faith in one God. They died *al kiddush ha shem*, for the sanctity of His name, choosing death over betrayal of the faith. Jews, therefore, who believe in a triune God are viewed as *meshummeds*, or traitors.

The passages in the *mezuzah* and phylacteries are capsulized reminders of the entire *Torah* (Law) and Divine Presence. Whereas they serve to remind the nation of their duty to observe all the commandments, these rituals are motivated by a love of God and an understanding of the unique relationship He has with the people called out for His Name. *T'phillin* further remind the Jew of the word *t'filah*, or prayer, and both words are derivatives of the root *palal*, meaning judgment. Israel was expected to testify to faith in the presence of Almighty God, and to us this is an opportunity for self-judgment and self-examination.

Establishing validity for interpreting the *Sh'ma* requires examination of the words God gave to Moses: *"Sh'ma Yisroel, Adonoi Eloheinu, Adonoi echad"* ("Hear, O Israel, Jehovah our God, Jehovah is One"). To better understand the sanctity and mystique of this profound statement, I interject that I (as were all Jewish youths) was taught to say: "Hear O Israel, the Lord our God, the Lord is One."

The name of God was never to be taken in vain, and the term *Adonoi*, or "Lord", was substituted for Jehovah. Some will only refer to God as *Ha Shem*, literally 'the Name'. You wouldn't pronounce His name or write it. As such, we learned to write G-d or L-rd.

Literally, the word *Eloheinu* is a plural form (Gods), and *echad* is a "compound one", or "unity", as opposed to an "absolute one". Since the Hebrew language has a word, *yachid*, which is an "absolute one", the more exact translation of the *Sh'ma* is: "Hear O Israel, Jehovah our Gods, Jehovah is a unity".

God, in telling Abraham to sacrifice Isaac, used the term *ben yachid*, clearly distinguishing him as his only son. Certainly God could have used *yachid* in the profession He gave to Moses, if He wished to convey His essence as an absolute One. Rather, the distinction here is that the Lord is a Unity, or United One.

Perhaps this conclusion can be understood better by examining similar construction. In Gen. 1:15 we read that *erev* and *boker*, evening and morning, were *yom echad*, "one day". Similarly, in Gen. 2:24 man and woman were to cleave to each other and become *basar echad*, "one flesh".

The opening words of the Bible are: *"B'reishis bara Elohim..."* ("In the beginning God created..."). The word *Elohim*, however, is the masculine plural, as are all Hebrew nouns ending with the *"im"* sound. For instance, *y'ladim* (boys) and *sh'kallim* (shekels [Hebrew coins]) are plural, as opposed to the singular *yeled* and *shekel*.

This is borne out as well in Ex. 20:3 with the admonition: *"Lo ye-yeh l'chah elohim acheirim al punav"*, "There shall not be to you other or strange gods before me." We see here that *Elohim* is properly translated as Gods, using the plural, with the adjective or modifier *acheirim* agreeing in the plural number.

Chapter 32 of Exodus recounts the story of the golden calf. When Moses delayed to come down from the mount, the people said,

"...make us gods..." (v. 2MT). The word here is *elohim*. Aaron responds (v. 4MT): "These are thy gods..."

When idols or strange gods are mentioned, *elohim*, the plural, is acceptable, but becomes singular in speaking (translating) of the Lord, Jehovah. One must conjecture that Moses, who wrote the Pentateuch, understood God as a triunity, and had no problem with the plurality of *Elohim*.

I was taught in Hebrew school that the plural, *Elohim*, speaks of the majesty of God, and can well understand why it would not ordinarily enter the mind of a Jewish person to question the use of the plural nouns and adjectives in speaking of God. Looking more deeply into the scriptures, however, sheds light on this subject. Note, as well, that *El*, or God, which is in the singular construction, could have been used. Had God referred to Himself as *El*, rather than *Elohim*, would one conclude that His majesty ceased to exist?

Noteworthy as well is the use of *Adonoi*, the plural construct of *Adon*, or "Lord". Thus, the plural construction of Gods and Lords allow and point to the understanding of more than one Divine personality.

The altar constructed by Jacob per Gen. 33:20 was called *"El, Elohei Yisroel"*, or "God, the Gods of Israel", further illustrating the understanding of a singular God, but manifested in plural form.

Going back to Gen. 1:26 we read: *"Va-yomer Elohim"* ("God said"), *"Na-aseh"* ("Let us make") *"adom"* ("man") *"b'tzalmeinu"* ("in our image") *"kidmuseinu"* ("and in our likeness"). Since God is speaking, the one(s) addressed as "us" appear to be of the same essence or nature. The singular nouns, "image" and "likeness" have a plural pronoun "our", so here, too, we are pointed to a plurality.

One more point by way of illustration is found in Gen. 3:22, where God exclaims that "...man is become as one of us..." *Elohim*, or God(s), is the speaker, so those who are *me-mehnu*, "like us", are of the same Divine nature and are equal with the Speaker.

At this point we can broach the subject of the Divine personality revealed as the Son, or, more accurately, God the Son. In dealing with this distinction it is helpful to understand the relationship between God and Jesus as revealed in the scriptures.

The criticism most frequently heard is that Jesus, Himself, refers to God as a separate entity, possessing knowledge He does not have. How then can Jesus be God? Here it is necessary to draw on the New Testament. Philippians 2:6-7 provides the best explanation: "...Who being in the form of God, thought it not robbery to be equal with God, but made Himself of no reputation, and took upon Him a form of a servant, and was made in the likeness of man..." Sonship, then, is the subjection by Jesus to a subordinate relationship with fleshly limitations in order to serve the purpose of God.

Though of Divine essence, and co-equal from eternity, Jesus clothed Himself with mortality to accomplish the objectives spoken of earlier. The role of the Kinsman-Redeemer necessitated coming in the flesh, and the vicarious atonement similarly demanded His physical surrender to death.

That which is deemed to be alien to Jewish thought can be re-evaluated in light of Hebrew scripture, beginning with Psalm 2. The ungodly ridicule the Lord, Jehovah, and His *Moshiach*, "Messiah" (Anointed). It is important to mention that the ancient synagogue and commentaries attached messianic interpretation, but this is not generally accepted by Judaism today. The modern view sees David as the anointed subject.

The One addressed as Messiah then speaks: "...Jehovah hath said unto me, 'My son art thou; I have indeed this day begotten thee' " (v. 7MT). In context we see not an event experienced by David, but end-time prophecy, when the heathen rage against the Messiah Who will not only overthrow these dissidents, but will be given " '...nations for an inheritance, and for thy possession, the uttermost ends of the earth' " (v. 8MT).

David never witnessed this in his lifetime, for surely this is a much broader scope of power and authority. Further distinction is drawn in the assertion: "Do homage to the son lest he be angry, and ye be lost on the way, for his wrath is so speedily kindled. Happy are all they that put their trust in Him" (v. 12MT).

We spoke earlier of the strenuous exception taken to the translation, "kiss the son", or "do homage to the son". This has been described to me as a most blatant and devious misuse of language to create messianic overtones. It is argued that *"bar"* is the Aramaic for "son", but the Hebrew that should be applied means purity; thus we are to pay homage to purity. Contrary to the exception taken, the ordinary content and context of the passage parallels paying homage to the same person addressed earlier: "Thou art my son." Aside from the fact that respected Jewish translators have agreed with the usage of "son", we see precedent in other passages as well.

Verse 2 of Proverbs 31MT asks the question: "What, O my son? and what, O son of my body? And what, O son of my vows?" All these are translations of the word *bar*, and no difficulty is presented by such rendering. In Ezra 5:1 as well, we read of prophecy by *Zechariah bar Iddo*, and there is no problem recognizing Zechariah as the son of Iddo. Attempts to attribute deceit and flagrant disregard for the language in Psalm 2, in view of all this, seems to be a smokescreen, and not a legitimate observation.

Psalm 2 elicits an understanding that the son will reign universally in righteousness, and all are to be accountable, that is, to pay homage (kiss the son). This in no way describes the much more limited reign of David when he sat on the throne. On the other hand, it coincides with other passages cited, such as Isaiah 11, which inarguably speaks of Messiah.

The attributes ascribed to the subject, here and in Psalm 2, force the conclusion that God, the Son, is in view. The theme of the Son, Inheritor of the throne, is carried through in Is. 7:11 and 9:6. Also, in discussing Micah 5:2MT, we saw that the origin of the ruler from Bethlehem was "...from olden times, from most ancient days." The emerging picture is that of the Son, Immanuel (God with us), the Everlasting Father, Whose goings forth are from everlasting. The Son then was with the Father from the beginning, and the "Sonship" transcends the traditional understanding of what that relationship represents.

According to the *T'nach* (the Hebrew scriptures: T=*Torah*, N=*N'viim*, C=*C'tuvim*), there are a number of incidents revealing the Divine presence. These are pre-incarnate manifestations of the Godhead Who later was born of a virgin and named Jesus (salvation). It is important to examine these references to the One called "the angel of Jehovah".

Genesis 16 makes reference to *Molech Jehovah*, the "Angel of Jehovah", Who appears to Hagar after she had fled from Abraham's wife, Sarah. The One called the Angel of the Lord reassures Hagar, Sarah's handmaiden, that upon returning and submitting to her mistress, her seed would be multiplied (she was about to give birth to Ishmael). Verse 13 records, "And she called the name of the Lord who spoke to her, Thou art an all-seeing God..." As defined here, the Angel, addressed as God, is a Divine presence.

In chapter 18 of Genesis, this Divine manifestation is seen by Abraham, for we read: "And the Lord (Jehovah) appeared to him by the oaks of Mamre..." Abraham addresses the visitor as "Lord", and He, in turn, responds that Sarah (although described as being old and stricken in years) was to give birth to a son. This causes Sarah to laugh (within herself), prompting: "And Jehovah said unto Abraham, Wherefore did Sarah laugh?...is anything too hard for Jehovah?" (vs. 13-14).

At the conclusion of this chapter we are told: "And Jehovah went away when He finished speaking with Abraham..." No doubt we can attribute all kinds of spiritual significance to these accounts, but coupled with the foundation laid, and the normal usage of the language, Abraham, Sarah and Hagar saw and spoke to a Divine presence (the pre-incarnate Jesus).

Moses, we learn from Exodus 3:2, encountered this Angel of Jehovah in Horeb: "And the angel of Jehovah appeared unto him in a flame of fire out of the midst of a bush; and he looked and behold, the bush burned with fire and the bush was not consumed...God called unto him out of the midst of the bush..." (vs. 2, 4).

Continuing in v. 6: "Moreover he said, I am the God of thy father, the God of Abraham, the God of Isaac and the God of Jacob. And Moses hid his face; for he was afraid to look upon God." Lest we still doubt the language which reveals a conversation between One called Jehovah, and the Angel of Jehovah, in the midst of a bush, verse 8 adds: "I am come down to deliver them (my people) out of the hands of the Egyptians..."

In Exodus 33 the Lord again appears to Moses (v. 11): "And Jehovah spoke unto Moses face to face, as a man speaks to his friend." During this conversation, Moses requests that if he found grace in God's sight, that the evidence would be that His Divine presence would accompany Israel, to which the response is: "And the Lord said to Moses, also this thing that thou hast spoken will I do...and he (Moses) said, Let me see, I beseech thee, thy glory. And he said, I will cause all my goodness to pass before thee...I will put thee in the cleft of the rock, and I will cover thee with my hand until I have passed by. And then I will take away my hand and thou shalt see my back parts; but my face shall not be seen" (vs. 17, 21-23).

The glory of God abode in the Tabernacle (*Mishkan*). This is the present tense of *shachan*, "to rest", "dwell" or "abide". In essence, the *Mishkan* or Tabernacle is the dwelling place of God's glory, and Moses, in these encounters, saw the *Shachana* or Shekinah glory of God.

As expressed in these passages, the Shekinah is a Divine manifestation of God, as is the Son, Angel of Jehovah or Messiah. God the Father is Spirit and cannot be seen, but this Person of the Godhead, God's Angel, was revealed and provides the explanation for what otherwise would be a contradiction. Year after year, we attend Passover *seders* and read from the Exodus story from the *Haggadah*. Here, too, the promise of God is that He would be present, not an angel and not a seraph! We submit that far from being a "Christian" concept, the triune manifestations are sound Hebrew theology.

In Judges 6:11 and 12, the "...angel of Jehovah sat under an oak which was in Ophrah, that pertained unto Joash, the Abiezrite, and his son, Gideon threshed wheat...And the angel of Jehovah appeared unto him, and said unto him, Jehovah is with you, thou mighty man of valor." This encounter provoked Gideon to exclaim, "Alas, O Lord God! for because I have seen an angel of Jehovah face to face. And Jehovah said unto him, peace be unto thee, fear not, thou shalt not die" (vs. 22-23). Having seen God, Gideon expected to be struck dead, but is assured that this was not to be the case. The only explanation, once again, is that the Divine manifestation is the member of the Godhead we now know as Jesus, the Messiah of Israel.

Judges chapter 13 describes a similar account with Manoah and his wife, Samson's parents, whereby they are confronted by the angel of Jehovah. Manoah's reaction, paralleling Gideon's, was (v. 22), "We shall surely die, because we have seen God."

Isaiah records in chapter 6:1: "...I saw the Lord sitting upon a throne, high and lifted up..." and he too declares (v. 5): "...Woe is me, for I am undone, because I am a man of unclean lips, and I dwell in the midst of a people of unclean lips; for mine eyes have seen the King, Jehovah of hosts." The preponderance of these accounts, and the consternation produced in the hearts of those having these revelations, are compelling. Our preconceived ideas must be re-evaluated in light of such disclosure.

Perhaps the passage that demanded my attention, like no other on this subject, is from the 48th chapter of Isaiah. The Lord is addressing Israel: "Hearken unto me, O Jacob, and Israel my called; I am He, I am the first, I am also the last" (v. 12). Since God alone is the First, Creator of all, there can be no doubt Who is speaking. Verse 13 continues: "Yea, my hand hath laid the foundation of the earth, and my right hand hath spread out the heavens; when I call unto them, they stand up together."

I doubt that any could object that God, the Creator, is the only One Who can make such a declaration. The prophetic vision goes on: "Assemble yourselves, all ye, and hear: who among them hath declared these things? He Whom Jehovah loveth shall perform his pleasure on Babylon, and his arm shall be on the Chaldeans. I, even

I, have spoken; yea I have called him; I have brought him, and he shall make his way prosperous" (vs.14-15).

Up to this point, God is reminding Israel that she has dealt treacherously (v. 8), but He would, for His Name's sake, refine them in the furnace of affliction (v. 10), and raise up a deliverer to "perform his pleasure upon Babylon", and that He would "make his way prosperous." It is increasingly obvious that the language brings to mind the Servant spoken of in many of Isaiah's writings, such as the 52nd and 53rd chapters, where we see: "The Lord has made bare his holy arm in the eyes of all the nations; and all the ends of the earth shall see the salvation of God...Behold, my servant shall deal prudently, he shall be exalted and extolled, and be very high" (vs.10, 13).

Examine carefully now the meaning of Is. 48:16: "Come ye near unto me, hear ye this; from the beginning I have not spoken in secret; from the time that it was, there am I, and now the Lord Jehovah hath sent me, and his Spirit." The One Who has been talking, revealing Himself as Creator, now says, "the Lord Jehovah hath sent me, and his Spirit."

Jesus, the exalted Servant, present with God from the creation ("Let us make man in our image"), is now being sent, along with the Holy Spirit, by Jehovah God, the Father.

Abraham, we saw in chapter 18 of Genesis, was visited by Jehovah in the plains of Mamre, and the Lord went on His way after revealing that Sarah would have a son in her old age. Sodom and Gomorrah were scheduled for destruction. In the next chapter, Lot is allowed to flee to a tiny city, Zoar; then (19:24): "And Jehovah rained upon Sodom and upon Gomorrah brimstone and fire, from Jehovah out of heaven." As in the account previously discussed, where Jehovah sent God and His Spirit, we see two persons addressed as Jehovah. In this instance, Jehovah, Who was conversing with Abraham, and then Lot, caused brimstone and fire to come down from heaven from Jehovah above.

We mentioned Proverbs 30 previously in dealing with the use of the word *almah*, or "virgin". Now we must go back to this passage to provoke a response to the question that is raised in v. 4: "Who was it that ascended into heaven and came down again?" (You may recall that in conjunction with Psalm 2, Psalm 110 and Hosea 5, a foundation was laid to establish Messiah's physical presence, rejection and return to the right hand of the Father, necessitating His coming in the flesh and His ascension.) "Who gathered the wind in his fists? Who bound the waters in a garment? Who set up the ends of the earth?" These rhetorical questions remind us of those God asked to humble Job when he presumed to question God's sovereignty, and there is no doubt here as to Whom it refers. "What is his name, and what is his son's name, if thou knowest it?" (v.4).

Arguably, all are, in a sense, sons of God, but the structure of these questions goes beyond such a response. The answer, rather, is the Child born, the Son given; the Wonderful One, Who, according to Is. 9:6, is not only a son, but co-equal and named by Jehovah: Almighty God, Everlasting Father and Prince of Peace.

Over the centuries there have been a number of false messiahs who offered hope to Israel. Each was a charismatic individual who garnered the support of a people desperate for deliverance. It is not surprising that a nation that has suffered so much, and for such a length of time, looks for the solution in anyone who promises to free them from tyranny and oppression. Each of these dynamic figures were, obviously, human, and had human frailties which led to their ultimate downfall.

The most renowned of these figures is known as Bar Cochba, "the son of a star". This name is drawn from the prophecy in Numbers, where we read about an incident involving the Moabites' threat to vanquish Israel, following their departure from Egypt. Balak, the king of the Moabites, was distressed that Israel successfully defeated the Amorites, and called upon the prophet, Balaam, to curse Israel. Every attempt to invoke such a curse was thwarted by God.

Finally, due to the Lord's intervention, Balaam replies: "How shall I curse whom God hath not cursed? or how shall I defy whom the Lord hath not defied?" (Num. 23:8). Continuing with the Divine vision, Balaam declares: "Surely there is no enchantment against Jacob, neither is there any divination against Israel; according to this time it shall be said of Jacob and of Israel, What hath God wrought! (v. 23). Then Balaam realized that it pleased the Lord to bless Israel, and extolled the virtues of the nation.

As the Holy Spirit grasped him in a viselike grip, Balaam fell into a trance and declared: "I shall see him, but not now; I shall behold him, but not nigh; there shall a star come out of Jacob, and a scepter shall rise out of Israel, and shall smite the corners of Moab, and destroy all the children of Sheth. And Edom shall be a possession, Seir also shall be a possession for his enemies; and Israel shall do valiantly. Out of Jacob shall come he that shall have dominion, and shall destroy him that remaineth in the city" (vs. 24:17-19).

Messiah was seen as the star out of Jacob, coming in power to deliver the oppressed people, and Bar Cochba fit the description for an eager population. Rabbi Akiva, a most famous and popular leader of the nation, supported Bar Cochba, so there was a feverish pitch of anticipation. Although this pseudo-messiah failed, as did all who preceded him, the expectation has been, and continues to be, that a human saviour is to redeem Israel.

In all my discussions with the Orthodox community, it remains the same. They regard it preposterous that the Messiah is to be a Divine, and not human, deliverer. As ever, the scriptures are not the basis for this decision, and quoting appropriate passages only elicits the response that those references have nothing to do with Messiah.

The most recent figure that stirred the hearts of those faithfully awaiting the Messiah was Rabbi Menachem Mendel Shneerson, the leader of the Lubavitch sect of Chasidim. Admittedly, he was ostensibly a prime candidate, in terms of the flesh, for he was a holy, dedicated, sincere, wise and committed human being. He was known within the community to perform miracles of healing, open barren wombs and to be a prayer warrior.

His passing in 1994 was a shock to the Lubavitch adherents, and even after his death and interment, the faithful remained at the grave, fully expecting his resurrection. In spite of the years that have gone by since, a large segment of the community still insists he is the anointed one.

Shneerson was responsible for maintaining an acute awareness among Judaism to watch for the coming of *Moshiach*. The cars of his followers bore bumper stickers, many with posters bearing his image, and "*mitzvah*-mobiles" and cars blasting Yiddish music, all calling attention to "We want Moshiach now!"

It has finally culminated in a statement, four years after his death, that the attempt to deify Shneerson is contrary to the tenets of Judaism, and a contradiction to his desire. The declaration was prompted by the suggestion of the more radical proponents of the Lubavitch, that Shneerson was indeed God, and could be prayed to.

Rabbi Shmuel Butman, who promoted the messiahship of Shneerson, has issued a carefully-worded statement which is intended to appease those who are looking to mend the schism that divides those who disagree with the preoccupation to identify this revered leader as the Messiah. However, Butman insists that the beliefs of the members of his sect are a very personal matter, so each is to make his own decision as to Shneerson's status, obviously leaving the door open.

Two extremely interesting points can be made from these recent events. First, although Judaism generally insists that Messiah is human and not Divine, it becomes apparent that some extremely informed and intelligent sources recognize that Messiah is indeed God. Secondly, we must see the inference that such a conclusion rests upon those prophecies that we insist talk of Messiah, but are not regarded as messianic by the modern commentators and synagogues. Simply put, the preconceived notions of Jews today have jaded their outlook, and it is popular to deny what was recognized as messianic prophecy by the ancient synagogue.

Since Messiah was to be Immanuel (God with us), and was called the Everlasting Father and Mighty God in Is. 9:6, it is good to see that at least some of our knowledgeable contemporaries draw similar conclusions. The person of the Godhead we call Jesus, the Messiah, is God in human form.

As a footnote to the Lubavitch recognition that Messiah is God, it must still be pointed out that Jesus remains abhorrent to Judaism. We may have areas of agreement, but we are continually confronted by those matters which prompt disagreement. Ironically, they may see Messiah as God, and give tacit approval to pray to Rabbi Shneerson, but overlook, or explain away, those verses of messianic prophecy that can in no way apply to the revered Rebbe.

According to Micah, our Messiah and Leader from everlasting is to be born in Bethlehem. Not only was Shneerson born in Poland, he never stepped foot in Israel. Any claims to his being from the tribe of David are suspect, as we have no way of proving one's lineage since the destruction of the Temple where the records were maintained.

In the next chapter we will talk about the timetable for Messiah's coming, and we have mentioned that His appearance would precede the destruction of the Temple.

6

THE SEVENTY WEEKS OF DANIEL

Very crucial to our putting together the pieces of the puzzle, is ascertaining the time element for Messiah's appearance. Judaism generally agrees, as do we, that we are not to speculate as to the time of Messiah's appearance. This, however, is associated with His return, and not His initial coming, which is recorded history.

Since the Temple was in fact destroyed in 70 A.D., and traditional Judaism fails to acknowledge Jesus' coming as fulfillment within the stipulated timeframe, are we to conclude that the scriptures are wrong or misinterpreted? Perhaps God changed His mind? The answer, we believe, is to be found in these famous but controversial verses in the book of Daniel.

It has been established that the scepter, or symbol of authority, was not to depart from Judah until the appearance of Messiah (Gen. 49:10). From this we deemed it appropriate to expect an appearance prior to 70 A.D., at which time the Davidic dynasty came to an abrupt end (with the destruction of Jerusalem). As stated, the genealogy records were destroyed with the Temple, and it would now be impossible to provide the credentials to identify Messiah from the house of David.

Daniel wrote that he understood "from the books" the number of years whereof the Lord came to Jeremiah, that He would accomplish 70 years in the desolation of Jerusalem (Dan. 9:2). It would seem that Daniel is referring to Jer. 25:9, 11-12, which indicates: "Behold I will send and take out all the families of the north, saith the Lord, and Nebuchadnezer, the king of Babylon, my servant, and will bring them against this land, and against the inhabitants thereof, and against all these nations roundabout, and will utterly destroy them, and make them an astonishment, and an hissing, and perpetual desolations...And this whole land shall be a desolation, and an astonishment; and these nations shall serve the king of Babylon seventy years. And it shall come to pass, when seventy years are accomplished, that I will punish the king of Babylon, and that nation, saith the Lord, for their iniquity..."

We know, too, Jeremiah wrote: "For thus saith Jehovah, after seventy years are accomplished at Babylon, I will visit you...then shall ye call upon me, and ye shall go and pray unto me, and I will hearken unto you...and I will turn away your captivity, and I will gather you from all the nations, and from all the places whither I have driven you...and I will bring you again into the place (Jerusalem) whence I caused you to be carried away captive" (29:10, 12, 14).

Daniel's vision in chapter 9 opens: "In the first year of Darius the son of Ahasuerus, of the seed of the Medes, which was made king over the realm of the Chaldeans; In the first year of his reign I Daniel, understood..." So Daniel had every expectation, based upon God's Word, that upon completion of 70 years of captivity in Babylon, his people would be restored to their homeland.

In verses 21, 22, 24 Daniel tells us that, as he was praying, "...the man Gabriel, whom I had seen in the vision at the beginning, being caused to fly swiftly, touched me...And he informed me, and talked with me, and said, O Daniel, I am now come forth to give thee skill and understanding...Seventy weeks are determined upon thy people and upon the holy city, to finish the transgression, and to make an end of sins, and to make reconciliation for iniquity, and to bring in everlasting righteousness, and to seal up the vision and prophecy, and to anoint the most Holy."

God knew that it would be necessary to explain to Daniel what he did not understand, so He dispatched His heavenly messenger to provide some insight. Gabriel warns Daniel to "...understand the matter, and consider the vision" (v. 23), and then proceeds to reveal: "Know therefore and understand, that from the going forth of the commandment to restore and to build Jerusalem unto the Messiah the Prince shall be seven weeks, and threescore and two weeks: the street shall be built again, and the wall, even in troublous times. And after threescore and two weeks shall Messiah be cut off, but not for himself: and the people of the prince that shall come shall destroy the city and the sanctuary; and the end thereof shall be with a flood, and unto the end of the war desolations are determined. And he shall confirm the covenant with many for one week: and in the midst of the week he shall cause the sacrifice and the oblation to cease, and for the overspreading of abominations he shall make it desolate..." (vs. 25-27).

Daniel fully expected total fulfillment; not simply the return from Babylon, but the end-time coming of Messiah the Prince, within 70 years. He did not realize that two separate restorations were in view. Gabriel was dispatched to help him understand that the latter-day fulfillment would involve not 70 years, but 70 "sevens", or 490 years. The Hebrew word *shevah*, or "seven", is used in the same sense as Lev. 25:8, which states: "And thou shalt number seven sabbaths of years unto thee, seven times seven years; and the space of the seven sabbaths of years shall be unto thee forty and nine years." Thus, although the end of the Babylonian captivity would come in 70 years, Gabriel wants Daniel to know that 70 sevens would pass before the final reconciliation of Israel, when the covenant blessing would be realized.

The fact that two different returns are in view is borne out when you consider that Jeremiah, after declaring the end of the captivity, went on to speak of a new covenant relationship that would be made with Israel and Judah. We will look at this more closely later, but for now we can see how Daniel's misapprehension is corrected. Six things were to take place, per the revelation of this vision:

1. To finish transgression: We have in view that, although Israel sinned in many ways, the national sin, the rejection of God's provision in Messiah, is to come to an end. This was spoken of earlier in reference to Hosea 5, when Jehovah declared that He would return to His place, until they acknowledge their offense and seek His face.

2. To make an end of sins: With the realization of Who Mes-

siah is, and the provision of the new heart promised in Jeremiah 31:31 and elsewhere, the nation of Israel will return to God and put an end to sin.

3. To make reconciliation for iniquity: The word here is *kaper*, from which we get *Yom Kippor*, or the "Day of Atonement". An annual atonement was demanded by Levitical law, and the end-time would bring about reconciliation by means of the atonement in Jesus.

4. To bring in everlasting righteousness: At the conclusion of the 490 years, God's holy regime will finally usher in a righteous reign. It is no accident that it says *tzedek olamim*, literally the "righteousness of the ages", since Jesus is our righteousness and will bring this to bear.

5. To seal the vision and prophecy: The will of God will have been made known, so there is no need beyond this point for further revelation.

6. To anoint the most holy: We know that, according to Zech. 6:12-13, the one called the Branch, the Messiah, is to come and "...build the temple of the Lord...", and "...he shall bear the glory, and shall sit and rule upon his throne; and he shall be a priest upon his throne..." Thus, the Temple is to be consecrated at this time, and God's glorious kingdom will be established.

According to the prophecy, the clock starts ticking with the commandment to rebuild Jerusalem. Isaiah 44:24, 26 speaks of such an occasion: "Thus saith Jehovah, thy redeemer, and he that formed thee from the womb...that saith to Jerusalem, Thou shalt be inhabited; and to the cities of Judah, Ye shall be built..." And, in verse 28, another servant of God is named, although not from His nation, but God will use whomever He chooses: "That saith of Cyrus, He is my shepherd, and shall perform all my pleasure: even saying to Jerusalem, Thou shall be built; and to the temple, Thy foundation shall be laid."

In the 45th chapter of Isaiah, God adds: (v. 1), "Thus saith Jehovah to his anointed, to Cyrus, whose right hand I have holden..." (v. 4), "For Jacob my servant's sake, and Israel mine elect, I have even called thee by thy name...though thou hast not known me." (v. 13), "I have raised him up in righteousness, and I will direct all his ways: he shall build my city, and he shall let go my captives, not for price nor reward, saith Jehovah of hosts."

Isaiah lived approximately 200 years before Cyrus, but God's vision reveals that Jerusalem and the Temple were to be ravished, necessitating their reconstruction. In glorious fulfillment, Ezra the scribe fills in the gaps: "Now in the first year of Cyrus, king of Persia...Thus saith Cyrus, king of Persia, The Lord God of heaven hath given me all the kingdoms of the earth; and he hath charged me to build him an house at Jerusalem, which is in Judah" (Ezra 1:1, 2). Not only did Cyrus issue this decree, but encouraged his subjects to accompany the Jewish captives who would return to rebuild the Temple to: "...help him (them) with silver, and with gold, and with goods, and with beasts, beside the freewill offering for the house of God that is in Jerusalem" (v. 4).

Some critics argue that Cyrus gave the decree to rebuild the Temple only, and do not start the countdown from this point. However, there is little doubt that the returning exiles had permission to build both the city and the Temple.

In the fourth chapter of Ezra we read about the opposition to the work, which resulted in a letter being sent that accused the Jews of insurrection (v. 12): "Be it known unto the king, that the Jews which came up from thee to us are come unto Jerusalem, building the rebellious and the bad city, and have set up the walls thereof, and joined the foundations." The letter asked that the records be searched which would provide evidence that this was: "...a rebellious city, and hurtful unto kings and provinces, and that they have moved sedition within the same of old time: for which cause was this city destroyed" (v. 15).

The work was successfully interrupted until the second year of Darius, king of Persia. Darius then checked the records and issued a proclamation (Ezra 6:7): "Let the work of this house of God alone; let the governor of the Jews and the elders of the Jews build this house of God in his place." Thus, the Jews were permitted to resume their work as was authorized by Cyrus' decree. That work, as shown in Ezra, involved not only the Temple, but the reconstruction of the walls and foundation of Jerusalem.

Since the prophecy is satisfied, we can calculate the year 536 B.C.E., the first year of the reign of Cyrus, as the start of the 70 years. If we count 69 sevens, we have 483 years, which would bring us to 30 C.E., the year of the crucifixion of Jesus. This fits the prophetic vision revealed to Daniel.

The first 7 "sevens", or 49 years (Dan. 9:25), the city was to be rebuilt in "troublous times". This fact is clear based upon the opposition recorded in Ezra, and which brought the work to a temporary halt. This period was to be followed by "threescore and two weeks" (62x7). According to Dan. 9:26, "And after threescore and two weeks shall Messiah be cut off, but not for himself..." Once again, prophecy was fulfilled with Jesus' execution by Rome.

There is to be a 70th week, or a final seven-year period to complete the 490 years spoken of by Daniel. However, the final period is postponed, dating from the crucifixion. God has set aside His dealing with Israel for a time, and this gap still exists for the time being. The counting will restart when the events Daniel spoke of in chapter 9, verse 27 take place: "And he shall confirm the covenant with many for one week: and in the midst of the week he shall cause the sacrifice and the oblation to cease, and for the overspreading of abominations he shall make it desolate, even until the consummation, and that determined shall be poured upon the desolate."

A world dictator, referred to as "the prince", will establish a covenant with Israel, and the countdown begins. After three-and-a-half years (the middle of the week, or seven-year period), the covenant will be broken. It appears that Temple worship will have been re-established, but violated at this point, since "the sacrifice and the oblation" will cease. This will usher in what is referred to as the "Time of Jacob's (Israel's) Trouble", or "the Great Tribulation". The last three-and-one-half years "shall wrath be poured out upon the desolate."

The time of the Great Tribulation, Jacob's trouble, is spoken of by Jeremiah in 30:4-7: "And these are the words that the Lord spake concerning Israel and concerning Judah. For thus saith the Lord; We have heard a voice of trembling, of fear, and not of peace. Ask ye now, and see whether a man doth travail with child? wherefore do I see every man with his hands on his loins, as a woman in travail, and all faces are turned in paleness? Alas! for that day is great, so that none is like it: it is even the time of Jacob's trouble; but he shall be saved out of it."

Suffering shall be so intense that it is described as a woman in childbirth, doubled over in anguish. At the conclusion, however, Jeremiah promises deliverance, for the Lord will come from Zion and turn away their ungodliness.

Isaiah refers to this same time (Is. 66:7-9): "Before she travailed, she brought forth; before her pain came, she was delivered of a man child. Who hath heard such a thing? who hath seen such things? Shall the earth be made to bring forth in one day? or shall a nation be born at once? for as soon as Zion travailed, she brought forth her children. Shall I bring to the birth, and not cause to bring forth? saith the Lord: shall I cause to bring forth, and shut the womb? saith thy God."

Isaiah indicates that before Israel went into labor, she brought forth. He then asks, "Who has heard such a thing?" Some deem this to be rhetorical, for the answer obviously is, "No one". It can also be seen as alluding to the birth of Messiah. Even before the Tribulation, preparation was made for the birth of Messiah, who would redeem Israel; so the birth precedes the travail of childbirth.

The next question is, "Shall a land be born in one day?" Again, before one gives birth there must be labor pains. Zion will suffer, and then bring forth her children. God will not shut the womb, but open the way to salvation.

When the 490 years are over, God's kingdom will be set up on earth. The Redeemer will come to Zion, as it is written, and Messiah's return will usher in the long-awaited reign of peace and justice. The return of the Lord is confirmed in the writings of Isaiah, who speaks as well of the restoration of the Edenic existence.

In chapter 61:1-2 we are told: "The Spirit of the Lord God is upon me; because the Lord hath anointed me to preach good tidings unto the meek; he hath sent me to bind up the brokenhearted, to proclaim liberty to the captives, and the opening of the prison to them who are bound; To proclaim the acceptable year of the Lord, and the day of vengeance of our God; to comfort all that mourn." The prophecy continues to describe the rebuilding of the waste places, and the blessing to follow. Although there is much suffering during the tribulation, God will take vengeance and wreak havoc upon the tormentors of His people. With the acceptable year of the Lord, in God's timing, will come the healing and restoration.

Daniel had recorded a vision earlier of four beasts which represented a succession of world leaders, or four kings of nations which were to come to power. He described how they would "make war with the saints" until the coming of the "Ancient of days" (7:21-22). According to chapter 7:9-10: "I beheld till the thrones were cast down, and the Ancient of days did sit, whose garment was white as snow, and the hair of his head like the pure wool: his throne was like the fiery flame, and his wheels as burning fire. A fiery stream issued and came forth from before him: thousand thousands ministered unto him...the judgment was set, and the books were opened."

There can be no doubt as to Whom Daniel sees in this vision. The Ancient of days, dressed in white (or righteousness), with hair like pure wool, seated upon a fiery throne, and bringing justice, can only be God. Adding to the vision (vs. 13-14): "I saw in the night visions, and, behold, one like the Son of man came with the clouds of heaven, and came to the Ancient of days, and they brought him near before him. And there was given him dominion, and glory, and a kingdom, that all people... should serve him: his dominion is an everlasting dominion, which shall not pass away, and his [Son of man's] kingdom that which shall not be destroyed."

Daniel 3 also recorded an incident whereby Nebuchadnezer had three of the Hebrew captives thrown into a fiery furnace. The king was astonished, for Shadrach, Meshach and Abednego alone were cast into the furnace, but the exclamation was: "...I see four men loose, walking in the midst of the fire, and they have no hurt; and the form of the fourth is like the Son of God" (3:25). Again, we are given confirmation of a Divine presence referred to as the Son of man, and the Son of God. He comes in the clouds of heaven, which takes it out of the realm of human endeavor, and gives weight to our understanding of a Divine Messiah. Only One with Divine attributes can have an everlasting kingdom which can never be destroyed.

These events should not be thought as strange, since they are consistent with recorded prophecy. Isaiah foretold (43:2): "When thou passest through the waters, I will be with thee; and through the rivers, they will not overflow thee: when thou walkest through the fire, thou shalt not be burned; neither shall the flame kindle upon thee."

God promised His Divine presence to accompany Moses and the children of Israel when they left Egypt, and He was there to bring them through the parted waters of the Red Sea. The waters did not overflow Israel, but the pursuing Egyptians were drowned. True to His promise, He brought the faithful Hebrew youths in Babylon through the fiery furnace, and the flames did them no harm.

God alone is our Redeemer, as shown in Is. 43:11-12: "I, even I, am the Lord; and beside me there is no saviour. I have declared, and have saved, and I have showed, when there was no strange god among you..." In this passage, the Lord continues to reveal how He always brought deliverance and performed miracles for His chosen people.

The testimony remains (vs. 21-22): "This people have I formed for myself; they shall show forth my praise. But thou hast not called upon me, O Jacob; but thou hast been weary of me, O Israel."

Israel was called to be a servant, and is greatly beloved of the Lord. They entered into a special covenant relationship and were given ample opportunity to prove themselves worthy. Time after time they failed, lapsing into sin and apostasy. They were severely punished and vanquished - scattered among the nations. It was up to the faithful Servant, Messiah, to appear before the Ancient of days, to come in the clouds of heaven, and to perform the will of God.

7

THE OVERVIEW OF MESSIAH'S CAREER

The preceding chapters offer quotes from many Biblical passages which provide a means to understand messianic prophecy. We have seen that an inherent sin nature renders man incapable of pleasing God, and that He alone is our righteousness. By coming in human form, Messiah would be able to identify with His creation, bear their iniquity, and reconcile lost humanity to a merciful God. Israel's Messiah would be God's salvation (*Yeshua*) to the ends of the earth, so both Jew and Gentile would be one in Him. Thus, the New Covenant relationship would be the internalization of these truths, as received by those with the new heart and new spirit.

The holy writings reveal that Messiah would be rejected by Israel in His first coming, and this would be the means through which the Gentile would come to faith in the God of Israel. The stone the builders rejected would then become the chief cornerstone, or foundation. God would pour out the Spirit of grace and supplication upon the house of Israel and the house of Judah, and we would look upon Him Whom we pierced and be in bitterness for having denied the Holy One.

Our portrait of Messiah was filled in by Isaiah, who revealed that He would be born of a virgin, and be Immanuel (God with us). He would be none other than the Wonderful Counsellor, Mighty God, Everlasting Father and Prince of Peace. Micah added that He would be born in Bethlehem; Zechariah told of his coming into Jerusalem riding upon an ass, and David gave us a graphic description of the mocking, scourging and crucifixion He endured. A timetable for His appearance was furnished by Daniel, and Moses wrote of those whose lives provided a glimpse of Messiah's career. He was revealed as the Branch by Jeremiah, the Root of Jesse by Isaiah, the Son of man and the Son of God by Daniel, and the Lord our Righteousness.

The Overview of Messiah's Career / 81

All these visions and pieces of a puzzle come together to reveal only one individual who, in the annals of history, met all the criteria. That which remains to be fulfilled - His return in power and the restoration of His creation - is as certain as all that which has already come to fruition. The Lord Whose Name is *Emuneh*, or "Faithful", will see to that.

As further indication of God's providing ample opportunity to know the truth, we now look at a prophetic overview of the messianic program revealed in Isaiah 49. We made some reference to portions of this material previously, as it fit into the topics then under discussion, but there is a much greater depth of information in this single chapter which enhances our understanding.

The message of Isaiah 49 is universal, for it opens: "Listen, O isles, unto me, and hearken, ye people, from far..." All the ends of the earth are to know the will of God, and the speaker addresses both Jew and Gentile by including those who had been far away, or those not privy to the covenant God made with Israel. The very nature of this summons to humanity reveals the speaker to be God, to Whom all are accountable.

Continuing, the Speaker refers to His origin: "The Lord hath called me from the womb; from the bowels of my mother hath he made mention of my name." Now that the Speaker has gotten our attention, He lets us know that not only was He called from the womb, but that was the point at which He would be named.

We commented earlier in this regard, so suffice to say that in reinforcing the messianic nature of the prophecy, attention is called to the womb of the mother. The nation Israel is routinely identified with the patriarchs, Abraham, Isaac and Jacob, but Messiah with the mother, an allusion to the virgin birth.

Verse 2 lays particular emphasis upon the mouth, for the words of this Speaker are of life-saving significance. We are to note carefully the qualities attributed to the One Who has called our attention: "And he hath made my mouth like a sharp sword; in the shadow of his hand hath he hid me, and made me a polished shaft; in his quiver hath he hid me..."

Comparing the mouth to a sharp sword further reinforces the Divine nature of the subject of this passage. The Word of God is powerful and is wielded as a sword to accomplish His objective. Like a two-edged sword, the mouth or Word cuts in two directions, and even hints at the two comings. The sword cuts to the quick, slicing away preconceived ideas and notions which keep us from truth. As the Word pierces our hearts to bring us to truth, so it is likened to a sword or even a scalpel used by a deft surgeon to save a life. In the second advent, the sword will cut in another direction, into the hearts of the King's enemies!

The reference to the sword or Word parallels as well the concept that was brought to our attention in Isaiah 11, which speaks of the stem of Jesse, the Branch, upon Whom would rest the Spirit of the Lord. According to 11:4: "But with righteousness shall he judge the poor, and reprove with equity for the meek of the earth: and he shall smite the earth with the rod of his mouth, and with the breath of his lips shall he slay the wicked." So here again we see the power of the Word displayed in slaying the wicked. The worlds were framed by the Word of God; He spoke, and brought them into being. With the breath of His lips He will destroy the evil, for the Word is indeed a two-edged sword.

Revealed as well as a polished shaft or arrow, the Speaker shows how He is perfectly fit to aim truly to hit the target. Our polished or sinless Messiah will enter the softened heart, bringing salvation. The hardened heart, not prepared to receive truth, will be pierced as well, but for destruction. Both the arrow and sword are hidden in the shadow of God's hand, but the vision is ever open to the seeker of truth. The implements of God are ready to accomplish His purpose and prosper where they are directed.

Israel is named as the servant in verse 3 of Isaiah 49: "And (he) said unto me, Thou art my servant, O Israel, in whom I will be glorified." We stand firm, however, that Jesus is the epitome of the faithful Servant, the perfect Israel Who comes to do the will of God.

God was to have been glorified in or by Israel, but we've examined how, time after time, there was failure. Since the purpose of God was not to be thwarted, it is in Messiah that He is now glorified. Man was created innocent, but it was not long thereafter that he was guilty of rebellion, and then fratricide. Israel was brought out of Egypt after seeing the mighty hand of God and numerous miracles. Moments later they were making a molten image, a golden calf, declaring "...These be thy gods, O Israel, which brought thee up out of the land of Egypt" (Ex. 32:4). Because of the apostasy of the nation, the Lord used Babylon to carry Israel into captivity. After the rebuilding of the Temple, the Lord once again destroyed the Temple of the apostate nation, forcing them into the *Diaspora* (Dispersion). A history of failure was to end in triumph, but it necessitated Messiah's total obedience and sacrifice, which glorified God.

We now see a prophetic vision of the seeming failure of the Servant who glorifies God. You will recall the reference in Genesis 3 where a temporary victory was granted to the seed of the serpent, for it was to bruise the heel of Messiah, the seed of the woman. On the tree of Calvary, according to Psalm 22, we saw a Messiah forsaken and crying out to God. In Isaiah 53 we saw that "All we like sheep have gone astray...but the Lord hath laid on him the iniquity of us all" (v. 6). And so the testimony here is: "Then I said, I have laboured in vain, I have spent my strength for nought, and in vain: yet surely my judgment is with the Lord, and my work with my God." (49:4).

The two advents are brought into view as well, for the first coming would seem to confirm the failure to which the Speaker alludes. Seeking Israel's immediate restoration, few looked for the suffering Servant who would take upon Himself the sin of the world to reconcile the lost to a holy God. To the casual observer, His strength was spent in vain, but the purpose of God was served even in Messiah's death.

In chapter 50, Isaiah goes on to reveal the greater plan: "The Lord God hath given me the tongue of the learned, that I should know how to speak a word in season to him that is weary: he wakeneth morning by morning, he wakeneth mine ear to hear as the learned. The Lord God hath opened mine ear, and I was not rebellious, neither turned away back. I gave my back to the smiters, and my cheeks to them that plucked off the hair: I hid not my face from shame and spitting. For the Lord God will help me; therefore shall I not be confounded: therefore have I set my face like a flint, and I know that I shall not be ashamed" (vs. 4-7).

The second part of Is. 49:4 then provides comfort for the Servant, and for those of us who identify with Him. Our judgment is with God, and He is our exceeding great reward. He recompenses good and evil, and we are to learn, as did our Messiah, to trust under every circumstance. The words of Is. 12:2-6 will yet be sung: "Behold, God is my salvation; I will trust, and not be afraid: for the Lord Jehovah is my strength and my song; he also is become my salvation. Therefore with joy shall ye draw water out of the wells of salvation. And in that day shall ye say, Praise the Lord, call upon his name, declare his doings among the people, make mention that his name is exalted. Sing unto the Lord; for he hath done excellent things: this is known in all the earth. Cry out and shout, thou inhabitant of Zion: for great is the Holy One of Israel in the midst of thee."

An unbiased reader would be hard-pressed to identify Israel as the servant, for it is Israel in view as the object, and not the subject, of the next verse: "And now, saith the Lord that formed me from the womb to be his servant, to bring Jacob again to him, Though Israel be not gathered, yet shall I be glorious in the eyes of the Lord, and my God shall be my strength" (Is. 49:5).

The Servant is called to bring Jacob again and to regather Israel. Jacob became known as Israel when he wrestled with God and prevailed. But even Israel, as all of us in a body of sin, need the imputed righteousness of our Messiah. Both Jacob and Israel symbolically are to be brought back to a holy God and redeemed, or spiritually restored.

The Overview of Messiah's Career / 85

Jacob left the land, fleeing from the wrath of Esau. Israel was scattered as well. God's Servant will bring them back in belief, and restore the land (which became desolate) too. In accomplishing God's objective, Messiah will be glorious, and, per verse 6, continue to fulfill the Lord's objective: "And he said, It is a light thing that thou shouldest be my servant to raise up the tribes of Jacob, and to restore the preserved of Israel: I will also give thee for a light to the Gentiles, that thou mayest be my salvation unto the end of the earth."

We can never overlook that Israel was to be a light to the nations, for God's mercy did not end with Israel. Thus it is not enough that Jacob and Israel are brought into the fold, but the Gentiles are to come to the light as well. At first blush, verse 7 repeats the account of Messiah's rejection, but in addition to revealing the attitude of the people and the nation, Jehovah offers confirmation that His Anointed will triumph: "Thus saith the Lord, the Redeemer of Israel, and his Holy One, to him whom man despiseth, to him whom the nation abhorreth, to a servant of rulers, Kings shall see and arise, princes also shall worship, because of the Lord that is faithful, and the Holy One of Israel, and he shall choose thee."

Assurance comes directly from Jehovah God, the Holy One, in addressing the Servant Who is abhorred. A picture similar to Isaiah 53 is painted to reinforce a Servant Who, unlike Israel, suffers in silence and puts Himself in total subjection to all authority. He is a servant of rulers now, but the time will come when He will be exalted; kings and princes will stand before Him. They will worship Him, Who for the present is despised and rejected of men, but chosen of God. The truth of Is. 28:16 will then be borne out: "Therefore thus saith the Lord God, Behold, I lay in Zion for a foundation a stone, a tried stone, a precious corner stone, a sure foundation: he that believeth shall not make haste." The stone rejected of the builders will indeed become the Chief Cornerstone, and (per Ps. 118:23): "This is the Lord's doing; it is marvellous in our eyes."

Many times the Word of God assures us of a basic principle: humble yourself in the sight of God, and He will exalt you in due time. A contrite spirit and obedience will ultimately result in blessing. This, too, is the promise to Messiah, and to us, as reflected in Is. 49:8: "Thus saith the Lord, In an acceptable time have I heard thee, and in a day of salvation I helped thee: and I will preserve thee, and give thee for a covenant of the people, to establish the earth, to cause to inherit the desolate heritages..."

Every aspect of this faithful Servant (unlike Israel) was complete submission to God, the Father. He was despised, ridiculed, smitten and hung on a tree. Yet, the assurance is, "I have heard thee...I have helped thee...I will preserve thee..." This is borne out in Psalm 20: "The Lord hear thee in the day of trouble; the name of the God of Jacob defend thee...Now know I that the Lord saveth his anointed; He will hear him from His holy heaven with the saving strength of His right hand" (vs. 1, 6). Again, in Psalm 21: "The king shall joy in thy strength, O Lord; and in thy salvation how greatly shall he rejoice! Thou hast given him his heart's desire, and hast not withholden the request of his lips...For thou hast made him most blessed for ever: thou hast made him exceeding glad with thy countenance. For the king trusteth in the Lord, and through the mercy of the most High he shall not be moved" (vs. 1-2, 6-7).

The grace of God is not given in vain. In times of adversity and frustration, the grace of God will see us through and be our encouragement. As joint heirs with Messiah, we receive this great inheritance. We can count on His hearing us, rely upon His help and trust in His preserving us.

The assurance of His comfort and provision is the fact of Messiah, Himself, being the covenant of the people. Not only is Jesus the mediator of the New Covenant (*Brit Chadasha*), but the very reality of the Covenant. The Old Covenant of the law was sanctified by the blood sacrifice, and the New Covenant as well, but now it is by the precious blood of the spotless Lamb.

Isaiah tells us the Messiah is the Prince of Peace (*Sar Shalom*). Micah not only revealed His place of birth in Bethlehem (5:2), but adds, in verse 5: "And this man shall be the peace..." We see in

Genesis that the Lord, Himself, was to provide the offering; in Isaiah, the Lord, Himself, would be our sign; now He is to be our blood covenant, the down payment and evidence of the promise of eternal salvation.

Psalm 95:7-8 cautions: "For he is our God; and we are the people of his pasture, and the sheep of his hand. To day if ye will hear his voice, Harden not your heart, as in the provocation, and as in the day of temptation in the wilderness..."

He hears and assures us in the acceptable time; now is that time, it is the time of salvation. All are cautioned, therefore, "If you hear His voice, don't harden your heart as they did in Moses' day, and provoked God."

The covenant is also to "raise up the land" and to "inherit the desolate heritages" (Is. 49:8). Sin separated man from God, but there was a curse upon the land as well. Thorns and thistles are the evidence of the curse, and man is to work by the sweat of his brow. Messiah is to reconcile sinful man to a holy God, and to restore the harmony of nature. The land is to be raised up from the waste and ruin and to become fruitful again. Once more it will be a land of milk and honey. Moses was our deliverer, but he was stopped from bringing the nation into the promised land. Joshua (symbolically *Yeshua*, or "salvation") picked up where Moses left off. The law came by Moses, but grace and truth by Jesus.

The children of Israel failed to keep God's commandments, and they were removed from the land that was apportioned under Joshua's direction. Now the land that is raised up by the new Joshua, *Yeshua*, will be reallocated to God's people who will inherit the desolate heritages. By the grace of God, Israel is to inhabit the land God gave them: that which was promised to Abraham, to Isaac and to Jacob.

Ezekiel was privileged to be shown by God how the land would be reapportioned in the last days (Ezek. 47:13-14, 21-22): "Thus saith the Lord God; This shall be the border, whereby ye shall inherit the land according to the twelve tribes of Israel: Joseph shall have two portions. And ye shall inherit it, one as well as another: concerning the which I lifted up mine hand to give it unto your fathers: and this land shall fall unto you for an inheritance...So shall you divide the land unto you according to the tribes of Israel. And it shall come to pass, that ye shall divide it by lot for an inheritance unto you, and to the strangers that sojourn among you, which shall beget children among you: and they shall be unto you as born in the country among the children of Israel; they shall have inheritance with you among the tribes of Israel."

You can read verses 15-20, which describe in detail the borders of the territories for each of the tribes, as it was done in the days of Joshua. From east to west and north to south, God has apportioned the land according to the tribes of Israel, and for the stranger (Gentile) who sojourns with them.

It is true that Israel returned to the land in 1948, but they are yet to possess all the territory that is described. More importantly, as a nation, they remain in unbelief: in spiritual darkness, and bound by sin. This will be dealt with, as Isaiah adds in 49:9: "That thou mayest say to the prisoners, Go forth; to them that are in darkness, Shew yourselves. They shall feed in the ways, and their pastures shall be in all high places." These words mirror much of what we already spoke of in quoting from Isaiah 42. Here we saw the Lord's Servant empowered by the Holy Spirit to bring judgment to both Jew and Gentile.

The Servant was to be sublimely gentle and meek, superbly righteous, the embodiment of the covenant to Israel and the light to the Gentiles. He was to open the blind eyes, bring out the prisoners from the prison and foster spiritual enlightenment.

In 42:19 we learn as well: "Who is blind, but my servant? or deaf, as my messenger that I sent? who is blind as he that is perfect, and blind as the Lord's servant?" These grandiose words cannot apply to Israel, but are a fitting description of the obedient Servant Who is endowed supernaturally to bring justice and peace.

In stark contrast, Israel is described as a people spoiled and robbed for having sinned against God (vs. 24-25): "Who gave Jacob for a spoil, and Israel to the robbers? did not the Lord, he against whom we have sinned? for they would not walk in his ways, neither were they obedient unto his law. Therefore he hath poured upon him the fury of his anger, and the strength of battle: and it hath set him on fire roundabout, yet he knew not; and it burned him, yet he laid it not to heart."

Continuing in chapter 43, the Lord expounds upon His holy nature and Divine purpose to redeem Israel, who are yet His people (v. 15): "I am the Lord, your Holy One, the creator of Israel, your King." "This people have I formed for myself; they shall shew forth my praise. But thou hast not called upon me, O Jacob; but thou hast been weary of me, O Israel" (vs. 21-22).

Now, in verse 25, we see once again that it falls to the mercy of God to do what Israel is incapable of doing: "I, even I, am he who blotteth out thy transgressions for mine own sake, and will not remember thy sins." The next verse is important to understand: "Put me in remembrance: let us plead together: declare thou, that thou mayest be justified."

Only through confessing their sin, and seeing justification in God alone, can there be forgiveness. "The just shall live by faith"! This was the vision of Habakkuk 2:4, and remains true to this day. Only in the Lord is righteousness.

The final verse of Isaiah 43 is a declaration by Jehovah, that He profaned the princes of the sanctuary, and gave Jacob to the curse and Israel to reproaches. He sent a blind and sinful people into captivity to learn a lesson. He then raised up Cyrus to issue the decree for Israel to return and rebuild the sanctuary. All this was not to have been in vain.

The prisoners are to go forth, and those in spiritual darkness are now to find release in the Lord. Sin had a hold on each of us, but the power of sin was broken when Jesus became sin for us and was nailed to the tree. Finally the curse is over, the prison doors have swung open and light has entered the hearts of those who have come to the truth. As Isaiah foretold in chapter 9, "The people that walked in darkness have seen a great light: they that dwell in the land of the shadow of death, upon them hath the light shined."

The second half of 49:9 conjures up a picture of Israel's Shepherd and His sheep. We've looked at this before in seeing how the political and spiritual leaders, or shepherds, failed, but the Good Shepherd, Messiah, steps forward to guide the flock. Jeremiah (50:6) called the nation "lost sheep", whose shepherds caused them to go astray to the point of forgetting their resting place. Ezekiel added (34:6) that the flock was scattered upon the face of the earth, and none did search after them. He prophesied, however, that they would not remain a prey to the heathen; they would not be devoured, and none would make them afraid.

The time would come when, "Thus shall they know that I the Lord their God am with them, and that they, even the house of Israel, are my people, saith the Lord God. And ye my flock, the flock of my pasture, are men, and I am your God, saith the Lord God" (Ezek. 34:30-31).

Both physically and spiritually, Messiah leads His sheep to good pasture, satisfying their hunger and thirst in both realms. They will come to the high places where they are exalted, or lifted up, by the hand of the Shepherd Who laid down His life for His sheep. Thus Is. 49:10-11 declares: "They shall not hunger nor thirst; neither shall the heat nor sun smite them: for he that hath mercy on them shall lead them, even by the springs of water shall he guide them. And I will make all my mountains a way, and my highways shall be exalted."

During the wilderness journey, the Lord provided for every need. In the midst of the wilderness He brought manna from heaven, water from the rock, and even flesh to eat. Clearly the miraculous nature of God's provision was evidence of His love and an encouragement. This supernatural provision is seen here as well.

Regardless of where He leads them, the flock will be nourished and protected from the heat of the sun. A merciful God will lead them to springs of living water and all their needs will be met. During the exodus, their feet didn't swell and their clothing didn't wear out. The nation will lack nothing at this time when the true Servant takes command once again.

The promise of verses 11 and 12 is: "And I will make all my mountains a way, and my highways shall be exalted. Behold, these shall come from far: and, lo, these from the north and from the west; and these from the land of Sinim."

These words remind us of the consoling narrative found in Isaiah 40, the beginning of which is known as the *Haftorahs* of Consolation (the portion read in the synagogue on the Sabbath). At God's direction, Isaiah brings words of comfort for Jerusalem (Israel), and promises to remove all the obstacles from their path. Valleys will be raised, mountains made low; the crooked made straight and rough places plain.

The voice crying in the wilderness will be for Zion and Judah to "...Behold your God! Behold, the Lord God will come with strong hand, and his arm shall rule for him: behold, his reward is with him, and his work before him. He shall feed his flock like a shepherd: he shall gather the lambs with his arm, and carry them in his bosom, and shall gently lead those that are with young" (Is. 40:9-11).

Our attention is again drawn to God, Who comforts, prepares the way, provides for His flock and Who is the true Shepherd of Israel. All exiles are to come back to Zion, from wherever they've been scattered: "Behold, these shall come from far: and, lo, these from the north and from the west; and these from the land of Sinim" (49:12). From all points of the globe will be the regathering, as foretold previously in Isaiah 11:12: "And he shall set up an ensign for the nations, and shall assemble the outcasts of Israel, and gather together the dispersed of Judah from the four corners of the earth."

The opening verses of this chapter, you may recall, explain that this will all be accomplished by the "stem of Jesse", the Servant Who is "the Branch". It is important to draw these parallels to keep in mind why the Servant is clearly Messiah, and not Israel.

A response is elicited from the people of God and from God's creation, for even the land is seen breaking forth into song, praising God for His glorious work of redemption (49:13): "Sing, O heavens; and be joyful, O earth; and break forth into singing, O mountains: for the Lord hath comforted his people, and will have mercy upon his afflicted."

It is interesting to note that God formerly caused His creation to testify against Israel. Chapter 1 of Isaiah is an indictment against a stubborn nation. "Hear, O heavens, and give ear, O earth: for the Lord hath spoken, I have nourished and brought up children, and they have rebelled against me. The ox knoweth his owner, and the ass his master's crib: but Israel doth not know, my people doth not consider. Ah sinful nation, a people laden with iniquity, a seed of evildoers, children that are corrupters: they have forsaken the Lord, they have provoked the Holy One of Israel unto anger, they are gone away backward" (vs. 2-4).

The heavens and earth could testify against Israel; the dumb ox and ass were inherently smarter. But through the completed work of the suffering Servant, the earth and mountains break forth into song and praise.

Prior to the heights of joy achieved by the atonement, Israel was in the depths of humility, per Is. 49:14: "But Zion said, The Lord hath forsaken me, and my Lord hath forgotten me." However, God never forgets, but orders circumstances and events to accomplish the greater objective. The assurance of verse 15 is: "Can a woman forget her sucking child, that she should not have compassion on the son of her womb? yea, they may forget, yet will I not forget thee."

Imagine, we envision the maternal instinct to be the epitome of love and nurturing. The love of God, however, is even stronger, and a far more excellent example of unmerited forgiveness and mercy. We see that it may be possible for a mother to forget, but our God cannot forget or fail us!

Chapter 31 of Jeremiah makes us aware of the New Covenant

relationship that replaced the Covenant of the law given on Sinai. By way of introduction to this new relationship, Jeremiah declares in vs. 3-4: "The Lord hath appeared of old unto me, saying, Yea, I have loved thee with an everlasting love: therefore with lovingkindness have I drawn thee. Again I will build thee, and thou shalt be built, O virgin of Israel: thou shalt again be adorned with thy tabrets, and shalt go forth in the dances of them that make merry."

We are assured of His everlasting love, on the basis of which He has drawn us to Himself. Slaves and animals were compelled to obey, but a loving God draws us. This is seen as well in Hosea 11:4: "I drew them with cords of a man, with bands of love: and I was to them as they that take off the yoke on their jaws, and I laid meat unto them."

Unlike the dumb animal that is forced into submission, God draws us by His love. The Servant has removed the bit and bridle and the yoke of oppression. We are to respond through grateful hearts, not because of force. Our forgiveness is manifest in being described as "O virgin of Israel" and "adorned with (thy) tabrets". We are new creations in Messiah; the old things have passed away, and all things are new. Sin has been dealt with and buried in the depths of the sea. We are, as it were, chaste virgins in God's sight, <u>as if we never sinned</u>!

This infinite capacity to extend mercy and forgiveness is further demonstrated in 49:16. May we remind you that Messiah came in the flesh to experience what God the Father could not do, being of spiritual essence. It was Messiah Who identified physically with His creation, and endured temptation, pain and suffering. His obedience to God in this subordinate role brought Him to Calvary. Being impaled to the tree, we see the prophetic fulfillment: "Behold, I have graven thee upon the palms of my hands; thy walls are continually before me."

What a testimony of obedience and love! An indelible impression is made by this piercing of His hands and feet as was foretold in Psalm 22. Our Savior's boundless capacity to forgive is confirmed as well by Isaiah in 54:7-8: "For a small moment I have forsaken thee; but with great mercies will I gather thee. In a little wrath I hid my face from thee for a moment; but with everlasting kindness will I have mercy on thee, saith the Lord thy Redeemer."

Upon granting forgiveness, God's plea is for us to respond in kind, and to forsake sin (55:7): "Let the wicked forsake his way, and the unrighteous man his thoughts: and let him return unto the Lord, and he will have mercy upon him; and to our God, for he will abundantly pardon."

Each of us thinks we have the answers, and we use all sorts of mental gymnastics to justify our preconceived ideas. This prompts the exhortation (55:8-9): "For my thoughts are not your thoughts, neither are your ways my ways, saith the Lord. For as the heavens are higher than the earth, so are my ways higher than your ways, and my thoughts than your thoughts." A humble and contrite spirit is required to take God at His Word, and, if need be, defy tradition.

Those who yield see the provision (49:17-18): "Thy children shall make haste; thy destroyers and they that made thee waste shall go forth of thee. Lift up thine eyes round about, and behold: all these gather themselves together, and come to thee. As I live, saith the Lord, thou shalt surely clothe thee with them all, as with an ornament, and bind them on thee, as a bride doeth."

We see that the children are to react in haste; that is, to speedily accomplish the Lord's objective in returning to the land of promise. Since now is the appointed time, there is to be no delay in responding.

Next we see that their eyes are to be lifted up to behold what is being done, for the eyes of Zion had been downcast. The years of oppression had taken their toll, and resulted in discouragement. In returning to Zion, the heads are to be held high.

Jehovah adds, "As I live", for this is an oath of affirmation. The desire of God is not to be stopped, and the security of His people is secure in that promise. The false teaching that the church is Israel is clearly erroneous, for Israel's restoration is assured by God's immutable oath.

The promise is clear. All who seek to harm God's children will be overthrown. Israel will make merchandise of their oppressors, and "wear" them as garments. We are reminded of a similar experience that took place upon the departure from Egypt: the children of Israel were told to borrow of the Egyptians jewels of silver and gold, and raiment.

Imagine, as they were departing, with no intent to return, their avowed enemies were to loan them these precious items! Absurd as it seems, the account in Exodus is: "And the Lord gave the people favour in the sight of the Egyptians, so that they lent unto them such things as they required. And they spoiled the Egyptians" (Ex. 12:36).

The translation from the Hebrew scriptures provides a more appropriate rendering, using the word "asked" (*vayishlu*), rather than "borrowed", since there was no intent to return what was given. One more miracle at the hand of God, for the wealth of Egypt was Israel's for the asking!

God gave Israel favor to receive what was required, and they "spoiled" or "emptied" Egypt. The years of service in bondage and rigor were now to be repaid. And that which was provided would be the means through which Israel would construct and adorn the wilderness Tabernacle.

The word translated as spoiled, "*natzal*", is used in Zechariah 3:2, and here it states that one is "plucked" from the fire. In other words, the reference is to that of one who has been spared. Perhaps the Egyptians who responded by providing the gold, silver and raiment were spared by displaying benevolence to the children of Israel.

Is. 49:19 adds: "For thy waste and thy desolate places, and the land of thy destruction, shall even now be too narrow by reason of the inhabitants, and they that swallowed thee up shall be far away." Narrowness always speaks of need and want, and, conversely, widening is the affirmation of God's blessing. That which was called a place of destruction and desolation is now too narrow to accommodate the hordes that will return to inhabit that which had been wasteland. The people will exclaim that the place is too narrow, for it is time now for the Lord to enlarge their estates, and give Israel their rightful possession to all the land described when He originally brought them out of Egypt.

Israel dwelled in Egypt, the Hebrew (*Mizraim*) being a "double straitness", or "extremely narrow". Oppressed physically and emotionally, this was the epitome of sin and being confined. God's purpose was to bring them to a place where they would enjoy wide borders, and this dream is now fulfilled.

We see also in Isaiah 54:1-6: "Sing, O barren, thou that didst not bear; break forth into singing, and cry aloud, thou that didst not travail with child: for more are the children of the desolate than the children of the married wife, saith the Lord. Enlarge the place of thy tent, and let them stretch forth the curtains of thine habitations: spare not, lengthen thy cords, and strengthen thy stakes; For thou shalt break forth on the right hand and on the left; and thy seed shall inherit the Gentiles, and make the desolate cities to be inhabited. Fear not; for thou shalt not be ashamed: neither be thou confounded; for thou shalt not be put to shame: for thou shalt forget the shame of thy youth, and shalt not remember the reproach of thy widowhood any more. For thy Maker is thine husband; the Lord of hosts is his name; and thy Redeemer the Holy One of Israel; The God of the whole earth shall he be called. For the Lord hath called thee as a woman forsaken and grieved in spirit, and a wife of youth, when thou wast refused, saith thy God."

Abraham began without a son to inherit his bounty. His wife, Sarah, was barren, but he trusted there would be a child of promise. The hope came to fruition in the birth of Isaac, which caused laughter and joy. Israel in captivity is likened to the barren Sarah, but now is a time to break into song after the years of being barren, or desolate.

An exhilarated mother, Zion will then declare (49:20-21): "The children which thou shalt have, after thou hast lost the other, shall say again in thine ears, The place is too strait for me: give place to me that I may dwell. Then shalt thou say in thine heart, Who hath begotten me these, seeing I have lost my children, and am desolate, a captive, and removing to and fro? and who hath brought up these? Behold, I was left alone; these, where had they been?"

Whereas Zion had been robbed, made a widow, and lost her children, the hopelessness has come to an end. This declaration, "Who hath begotten me these, seeing I have lost my children?" is akin to Sarah's laughter when her barren womb was opened. The time of exile is over, and an astonished but grateful mother (Jerusalem) is overwhelmed by God's bountiful provision, and exclaims, "I was left alone; these, where had they been?"

There will be a remarkable turn of events when Israel is brought back into the land. In a reversal of roles, those who were the oppressors will be brought into subjection (Is. 49:22): "Thus saith the Lord God, Behold, I will lift up mine hand to the Gentiles, and set up my standard to the people: and they shall bring thy sons in their arms, and thy daughters shall be carried upon their shoulders." The picture is that of God raising His hand and beckoning or calling Israel to return. Messiah is the ensign or standard around whom they would rally, as established earlier (Is. 11:10-12): "And in that day there shall be a root of Jesse, which shall stand for an ensign of the people; to him shall the Gentiles seek: and his rest shall be glorious. And it shall come to pass in that day, that the Lord shall set his hand again the second time to recover the remnant of his people, which shall be left, from Assyria, and from Egypt, and from Pathros, and from Cush, and from Elam, and from Shinar, and from Hamath, and from the islands of the sea. And he shall set up an ensign for the nations, and shall assemble the outcasts of Israel, and gather together the dispersed of Judah from the four corners of the earth."

Israel will be carried upon the shoulders of the nations which formerly carried them into captivity. The imagery is that of children being tenderly carried in the nurturing arms or bosom in a protective manner. In 49:23 we see the exaltation of Israel, for even the kings and queens of the nations shall be in obeisance: "And kings shall be thy nursing fathers, and their queens thy nursing mothers: they shall bow down to thee with their face toward the earth, and lick up the dust of thy feet; and thou shalt know that I am the Lord: for they shall not be ashamed that wait for me."

Now is the time for the humbling of the proud, as they "lick the dust" and see the mighty hand of God, Who vindicates His people who trust Him. What a glorious picture of the Lord working His will (Is. 60:14-16): "The sons also of them that afflicted thee shall come bending unto thee; and all they that despised thee shall bow themselves down at the soles of thy feet; and they shall call thee, The city of the Lord, The Zion of the Holy One of Israel. Whereas thou hast been forsaken and hated, so that no man went through thee, I will make thee an eternal excellency, a joy of many generations. Thou shalt also suck the milk of the Gentiles, and shalt suck the breast of kings: and thou shalt know that I the Lord am thy Saviour and thy Redeemer, the mighty One of Jacob."

These same thoughts are mirrored in the closing verses of chapter 49 (vs. 25-26): "But thus saith the Lord, Even the captives of the mighty shall be taken away, and the prey of the terrible shall be delivered: for I will contend with him that contendeth with thee, and I will save thy children. And I will feed them that oppress thee with their own flesh; and they shall be drunken with their own blood, as with sweet wine: and all flesh shall know that I the Lord am thy Saviour and thy Redeemer, the mighty One of Jacob."

In conclusion, Israel is justified and restored to the Lord, and the enemies of God's people will drink their own blood and eat their own flesh. The world will yet learn that "No weapon that is formed against thee shall prosper..." (Is. 54:17). Haman will hang upon the gallows he built for Mordechai, and the pharaohs of the world will see their own firstborn drown in the sea intended for the sons of Israel!

8

PSALM 45

As with Isaiah 49, a beautiful messianic overview gives us insight into the career of our Savior. Whereas the ancient synagogue saw the messianic implication, modern commentaries attribute these verses to David's son, Solomon, and the wedding described here, as Solomon's marriage to Pharaoh's daughter. A closer examination will allow the reader to decide.

By way of introduction, we first see that the writer is constrained by an overflowing heart (v. 1): "My heart is inditing a good matter: I speak of things which I have made touching the king: my tongue is the pen of a ready writer."

It is written that "...out of the abundance of the heart, the mouth speaketh" (Matt. 12:34). The heart of the writer is swelling to overflowing with an appreciation and love for his king, the promised Messiah and Savior. It is all but impossible to remain silent when the child of God is touched by the realization of His glorious ways.

To further illustrate that he is prompted by the Holy Spirit, the psalmist now indicates that he is but speaking the words put into his heart and mouth by God. The book of Numbers records an incident whereby the Gentile prophet, Balaam, was called by Balak, the king of the Moabites to curse Israel. God took control of the situation, and Israel wound up with a blessing. When Balak complained to Balaam that he did not satisfy the purpose for his being hired, Balaam said that he could only speak as the Lord put the words into his mouth. Here, too, that which is spoken by the writer of the 45th Psalm is Divinely inspired.

Lest there by any wrong interpretation, we are now shown that the object of these gracious words is clearly unique (v. 2): "Thou art fairer than the children of men: grace is poured into thy lips: therefore God hath blessed thee for ever." He is seen here as greater than mere men, for He is Immanuel, (God with us); *Avi Ad*, the Everlasting Father; *El Gibbor*, Mighty God. The Hebrew *ya-phee-tah* is rendered "more fair", but is actually a compound form of the word "beautiful". Words are repeated to suggest a doubling or perfection. For instance, *shalom, shalom* is translated as "perfect peace". Here, the compounded word suggests "perfect beauty".

This describes more than the physical, for the spiritual beauty and Divine nature are called into view. In both Psalms and Chronicles we are told a number of times to worship the Lord in the beauty of His holiness.

Special attention is drawn to the mouth of the king, for grace is poured into his lips. His words are gracious, bringing a message of hope and Divine favor for a sin-laden world. When Jesus taught in the synagogue in Galilee, it is recorded that the people "...wondered at the gracious words which proceeded out of his mouth" (Luke 4:22). One can only add that He is therefore blessed forever.

This king is then addressed in terms attributable to God (vs. 3-4): "Gird thy sword upon thy thigh, O most mighty, with thy glory and thy majesty. And in thy majesty ride prosperously because of truth and meekness and righteousness; and thy right hand shall teach thee terrible things."

Not only is the Word of God a two-edged sword, but the Word is a symbol of justice and judgment. Grace is available for the seeker of truth, but the sword will cut into the heart of the King's enemies. The heathen rages against the Lord and His Anointed (Messiah), but Psalm 2 assures us that the Lord will have them in derision. The Mighty God will indeed prosper and be glorious.

"Who is this King of glory? The Lord strong and mighty, the Lord mighty in battle. Lift up your heads, O ye gates; even lift them up, ye everlasting doors; and the King of glory shall come in. Who is this King of glory? The Lord of hosts, he is the King of glory" (Ps. 24:8-10). Messiah came in human form, and we beheld His humanity and perfect subjection to all earthly authority. There is a time coming when we shall see Him in His glory and power. With His coming will be truth and justice for the meek. Our hope and vindication is of the Lord.

The fifth verse of Psalm 45 provides a glimpse of the battlefield (v. 5): "Thine arrows are sharp in the heart of the king's enemies; whereby the people fall under thee." The arrows launched by the Mighty One pierce the hearts of the enemy, and bodies are seen falling to the earth. We learned previously that the arrows are polished, or are perfectly clean, to aim true. They will not miss their targets.

All of God's enemies, and those of His Anointed, will pay the ultimate price. As foreseen is Isaiah 11, Messiah is to slay the wicked with the breath of His lips, and smite the earth with the rod of His mouth. Righteousness will then prevail.

Upon subduing His enemies, Messiah is seen on the throne where He belongs (v. 6): "Thy throne, O God, is for ever and ever: the sceptre of thy kingdom is a right sceptre." We are not to forget that the kings of Israel temporarily sat upon the Lord's throne. He is the rightful possessor, and now the Eternal One is to inherit the throne forever. Messiah is not only a Priest forever, after the order of Melchizedek (Ps. 110:4), but truly *Melech-Tzedek*, the "Righteous King".

In His Divine glory and majesty, the Mighty One ascends to the throne. The declaration is *Cee-sacha Elohim*: "Thy throne, O God, is for ever and ever." Messiah is addressed as God, but the Hebrew is translated as "Thy throne, given of God, endureth forever." The words, "given of", however, do not appear in the text. It appears that the translation is altered to suit the preconceived notion that does not recognize the deity of Messiah.

Zechariah had written (9:9): "Rejoice greatly, O daughter of Zion; shout, O daughter of Jerusalem: behold, thy King cometh unto thee: he is just, and having salvation; lowly, and riding upon an ass, and upon a colt the foal of an ass." The King, also known as the Servant called the Branch, has come to dwell in our midst and to establish His throne. In His first appearance He was meek and lowly, seated upon a donkey. In His second coming, He will be seated on the throne of David. "I have made a covenant with my chosen, I have sworn unto David my servant, Thy seed will I establish for ever, and build up thy throne to all generations...For the Lord is our defence; and the Holy One of Israel is our king...He shall cry unto me, Thou art my father, my God, and the rock of my salvation. Also I will make him my firstborn, higher than the kings of the earth" (Ps. 89:3-4, 18, 26-27).

It is confirmed in Psalm 45 that Messiah's throne is forever, and His scepter, or rule, is with righteousness. He alone is both righteous and eternal. In Is. 9:7, in speaking of the Mighty God and Everlasting Father, we saw: "Of the increase of His government and peace there shall be no end, upon the throne of David, and upon his kingdom, to order it, and to establish it with judgment and with justice from henceforth even for ever. The zeal of the Lord of hosts will perform this."

Only He can bring the promise of eternal peace and justice. All born of the flesh have sinned. Deceitful hearts, as described by Jeremiah, are destined to sin. The hallmark of Messiah's excellence, however, is seen in verse 7 of Psalm 45: "Thou lovest righteousness, and hatest wickedness: therefore God, thy God, hath anointed thee with the oil of gladness above thy fellows."

Sin could be conquered only by the One Who knew no sin. Taking upon Himself the sin of humanity, and imputing His righteousness to us, is the proof positive of hating wickedness and loving righteousness. Israel compromised with sin; the best of us have failed as well. He set His face as a flint, and never wavered in facing this issue with uncompromising holiness.

The consequence was quoted earlier, but is supremely relevant here: "...therefore God, thy God, hath anointed thee with the oil of gladness above thy fellows." God, the Son, is anointed by God the Father, with God, the Holy Spirit. According to Isaiah 61:1, He was anointed with the Spirit to bring good tidings (the Good News) to the meek. We note, as well, that He is seen set apart, or "above thy fellows". He Who is "fairer than the children of men" is unique.

Though manifest in the flesh, He is a product of the Holy Spirit, and of Divine essence.

Jeremiah 31 speaks of the New Covenant that the Lord will make with His people. They had violated the Old Covenant (the *Torah*, or "Law"), "...although I was an husband unto them, saith the Lord" (v. 2). Isaiah refers to this relationship several times, as does Hosea in 2:19-20: "...yea, I will betroth thee unto me in righteousness, and in judgment, and in lovingkindness, and in mercies. I will even betroth thee unto me in faithfulness: and thou shalt know the Lord."

The psalmist now picks up this theme and describes the wedding between Messiah and His bride, the congregation of believers: "All thy garments smell of myrrh, and aloes, and cassia, out of the ivory places, whereby they have made thee glad. Kings' daughters were among thy honourable women: upon thy right hand did stand the queen in gold of Ophir. Hearken, O daughter, and consider, and incline thine ear; forget also thine own people, and thy father's house; So shall the king greatly desire thy beauty: for he is thy Lord; and worship thou him" (Ps. 45:8-11).

As the Groom is holy, so are His garments. They are pure and fragrant, beautifully scented, a sweet savor in the nostrils of God. Myrrh, aloes and cassia are mentioned. We know that myrrh was a product of the land of Canaan, and a fragrant gum. It was one of the compounds used in the sacred anointing oil (Ex. 30:23), used for perfume (Esther 2:12), and brought as a gift by the wise men to Jesus. It was even used for His burial preparation after the crucifixion.

Aloes were used for perfume as well (Prov. 7:17), and for burial preparation. Cassia was an aromatic plant mentioned in Ezekiel and specified as an ingredient for the sacred anointing oil per Ex. 30:24. But, most fittingly, they describe the beauty and holiness of the Bridegroom. In the Song of Solomon, they are used to paint a loving and romantic picture of the relationship between the bride and groom.

Throughout the Old Testament we read of these same sweet fragrances and of the ivory palaces. Splendor and whiteness, or purity, is symbolized by the precious ivory inlaid upon the walls of the king's palace. In the Hebrew translation of Psalm 45 we read: "...out of the palaces of ivory have they made thee joyful with the sound of music." Joyful music upon stringed instruments is played before the king and his bride, for it is written: "Make a joyful noise unto God, all ye lands: Sing forth the honour of his name: make his praise glorious" (Ps. 66:1-2).

In attendance we see the daughters of kings and the queen (the bride). The daughters of kings represent the nations of the world who have come to faith and pay homage. Although the heathen at one time raged against the Lord's Anointed, having the imputed righteousness of Jesus, they are now described as "honorable women". In the Hebrew translation of Psalm 45 we read: "Kings' daughters are among those dear (or precious) to thee."

At the right hand of the king is the queen, restored Israel, adorned in gold. Once the harlot, she is now presented as a chaste virgin, without spot or wrinkle. Hosea chapter 2 provides much insight here as well. Hosea was instructed to take a whore for a wife to symbolize the spiritual fornication of Israel in being unfaithful to God. The children of this relationship were to be called *lo-ruchamah* ("not pitied") and *lo-ammi* ("not my people"), which again reflected how God looks at unfaithfulness.

At this point the Lord instructs Hosea to admonish the nation which has played the harlot, and failed to recognize all God had done for them. It was His intent to: "...allure her, and bring her into the wilderness, and speak comfortably unto her. And I will give her vineyards from thence, and the valley of Achor for a door of hope: and she shall sing there, as in the days of her youth, and as in the day when she came up out of the land of Egypt. And it shall be at that day, saith the Lord, that thou shalt call me Ishi; and shalt call me no more Baali...And in that day will I make a covenant for them with the beasts of the field, and with the fowls of heaven, and with the creeping things of the ground: and I will break the bow and the sword and the battle out of the earth, and will make them to lie down safely" (Hos. 2:14-16, 18).

God's desire is to promote blessings, but He can't reward deviant behavior. Forsaking sin would allow restoration, however, so that the relationship could become what was originally intended: "And I will betroth thee unto me for ever; yea, I will betroth thee unto me in righteousness, and in judgment, and in lovingkindness, and in mercies. I will even betroth thee unto me in faithfulness: and thou shalt know the Lord. And it shall come to pass in that day, I will hear, saith the Lord, I will hear the heavens, and they shall hear the earth; And the earth shall hear the corn, and the wine, and the oil; and they shall hear Jezreel. And I will sow her unto me in the earth; and I will have mercy upon her that had not obtained mercy; and I will say to them which were not my people, Thou art my people; and they shall say, Thou art my God." (vs. 19-23).

Israel had played the harlot, but now, justified, she stands as the queen, arrayed in gold. She is betrothed forever, by the grace of God, and seen as a chaste virgin. Messiah's kingdom upon earth, as sworn to Abraham, Isaac and Jacob, is to be witnessed. This is demanded by God's inviolate promise to His people.

As the bride takes her place at the side of the groom, we see the instruction that is provided: "Hearken, O daughter, and consider, and incline thine ear; forget also thine own people, and thy father's house; So shall the king greatly desire thy beauty: for he is thy Lord; and worship thou him" (vs. 10-11).

This address typically opens with the word *Sh-mi*, or, "to pay attention" to a most important principle. She is told as well, *oo-ree*, "to see", "look carefully" or give thoughtful consideration to that which is spoken. Further emphasis is added in that her ear is to be inclined. One can practically envision an attentive and obedient respondent, leaning over, intent upon catching every word spoken.

A young woman, leaving home, has been nurtured and protected by a father who has had responsibility for her well-being. At this point her former life is to be left behind. The time has come to move on.

In the same sense, the call of God is a call to separation and rearrangement of priorities. Abraham, the first Hebrew, was asked to set an example for all who would enter into a relationship with the Lord. He was to leave country and kindred, to become totally dependent upon God and no one else. Each of us must do likewise, recognizing our responsibility to this new relationship, convinced that our Maker and Husband is prepared to accept responsibility from this point forward. That conviction includes supreme confidence in the One Who loves us, and trust that He is able to meet every need.

It is not easy to forsake all; old habits, customs and relationships are hard to deny. But if we divide our loyalties, or in any way compromise our total dependence upon God, the relationship suffers. We do not deny our heritage and traditions, insofar as they provided a means of growth and introduction to God's ways. However, He will now teach us all we have to know. Bringing old baggage will only cause confusion.

A most glorious promise is the consequence of our obedience to this difficult but necessary instruction. He will desire our beauty, or be motivated to vindicate the trust we put in Him. We are repaid in kind with His undivided love and affection.

Our comprehension is limited in attempting to understand how God could desire us and want to meet our every need. A marriage relationship is the closest parallel that can suggest such intimacy and love, within our fleshly limitations. This analogy, however, provides a frame of reference, and we see the mutuality of a relationship that brings us to our knees in adoration. We love Him because He first loved us. Therefore, we now accede to his Lordship and worship Him with hearts overflowing with love and awe.

According to verse 12, those in attendance are to pay homage, for Israel is restored to the place intended by God. No longer the tail, but the head, those who treated the nation with cruelty and disrespect will now honor her. "And the daughter of Tyre shall be there with a gift; even the rich among the people shall intreat thy favour. The king's daughter is all glorious within: her clothing is of wrought gold" (45:12-13).

Among the nations of the world seeking Israel's favor, and bringing gifts, is Tyre. She is a symbol of pride and opulence, destined to be overthrown, as foretold in Isaiah 23:8, 10-11: "Who hath taken this counsel against Tyre, the crowning city, whose merchants are princes, whose traffickers are the honourable of the earth...Pass through thy land as a river, O daughter of Tarshish: there is no more strength. He stretched out his hand over the sea, he shook the kingdoms: the Lord hath given a commandment against the merchant city, to destroy the strong holds thereof."

Other passages similarly foretold this turn of events which will bring a role reversal, such as Joel 3:4-8: "Yea, and what have ye to do with me, O Tyre, and Zidon, and all the coasts of Palestine? Will ye render me a recompense? And if ye recompense me, swiftly and speedily will I return your recompense upon your own head; Because ye have taken my silver and my gold, and have carried into your temples my goodly pleasant things: The children also of Judah and the children of Jerusalem have ye sold unto the Grecians, that ye might remove them far from their border. Behold, I will raise them out of the place whither ye have sold them, and will return your recompense upon your own head: And I will sell your sons and your daughters into the hand of the children of Judah, and they shall sell them to the Sabeans, to a people far off: for the Lord hath spoken it."

With the certainty of a God Who cannot fail, Isaiah 60 now is brought to fruition (vs. 10, 12, 15-16): "And the sons of strangers shall build up thy walls, and their kings shall minister unto thee: for in my wrath I smote thee, but in my favour have I had mercy on thee...For the nation and kingdom that will not serve thee shall perish; yea, those nations shall be utterly wasted...Whereas thou hast been forsaken and hated, so that no man went through thee, I will make thee an eternal excellency, a joy of many generations. Thou shalt also suck the milk of the Gentiles, and shalt suck the breast of kings: and thou shalt know that I the Lord am thy saviour and thy redeemer, the mighty One of Jacob."

All nations are to honor God's chosen people, as Messiah and His bride, Israel, bask in His glory. That which has been left behind will be insignificant now as joyful Israel, once humbled, is now elevated. "The king's daughter is all glorious within: her clothing is of wrought gold. She shall be brought unto the king in raiment of needlework: the virgins her companions that follow her shall be brought unto thee" (Ps. 45:13-14).

Israel is pictured here most gloriously in clothing wrought with gold. Gold speaks of royalty and purity, for she is seen justified and fit to come into the presence of Melchizedek, the righteous king. The needlework or embroidery hints at the garments described as being worn by the high priest, suggestive of the heights to which the nation is now raised. Also coming into the presence of the king are virgins, her companions, or the kings' daughters previously mentioned, who are among the honorable women. Our Lord and King loves all nations and peoples, and all are justified and glorified in His righteousness.

Limitations exist in the human realm, and polygamy is not approved by God. Not being bound in the spiritual realm, however, He, Who is no respecter of persons, has love for all; for He is Lord of all. It is His desire that none perish and all share in His reflected glory.

Israel is called God's firstborn, and had a unique calling and relationship. We are to realize that as a parent loves all children, so the Lord equally loves all His creation. Each of His daughters is seen as a chaste virgin (cleaned up) and brought near. The concluding verses of the psalm foretell the results of this union (vs. 15-17): "With gladness and rejoicing shall they be brought: they shall enter into the king's palace. Instead of thy fathers shall be thy children whom thou mayest make princes in all the earth. I will make thy name to be remembered in all generations: therefore shall the people praise thee for ever and ever."

Israel's patriarchs were men of noble character and faith. Many of the blessings we enjoy are the result of the promises made to them. Yet, instead of the fathers, the offspring of King Messiah and His bride are to be princes in the earth. Not simply living in the past, a wonderful future is predicted.

In the beginning, the bride was instructed to forget her father's house. Much is sacrificed when we let go and move forward into the unknown. The only known factor is the measure of God's love and His goodness. Trust in a holy God is vindicated, and fruit ensues, eclipsing what was left behind.

What can be added, but to be ever-grateful and committed to praising and glorifying the Name of our Lord? He is given a Name above every name, and at the Name of Jesus every knee must bow and every tongue confess that He is Lord, to the glory of God, the Father.

Psalm 72:20 states: "The prayers of David the son of Jesse are ended", bringing David's final words to an end. His words sum up for us all our expression of adoration and awareness of Who He is (72:17-19): "His name shall endure for ever: his name shall be continued as long as the sun: and men shall be blessed in him: all nations shall call him blessed. Blessed be the Lord God, the God of Israel, who only doeth wondrous things. And blessed be His glorious name for ever: and let the whole earth be filled with his glory. Amen, and Amen."

9

THE FEASTS OF JEHOVAH

A close look at the feasts of Jehovah is in order, for they are the shadow of things to come. Before we probe the festivals, however, it is appropriate to examine the Sabbath and its relationship to the believer. Is there justification for worshipping on Sunday, or is it, as is claimed by some, a counterfeit of the true Sabbath, intended to be Saturday, the seventh day of the week?

Leviticus 23:1-4 makes it clear that the understanding and observance of the Sabbath is to be our first consideration: "And the Lord spake unto Moses, saying, Speak unto the children of Israel, and say unto them, Concerning the feasts of the Lord, which ye shall proclaim to be holy convocations, even these are my feasts. Six days shall work be done: but the seventh day is the sabbath of rest, an holy convocation; ye shall do no work therein: it is the sabbath of the Lord in all your dwellings. These are the feasts of the Lord, even holy convocations, which ye shall proclaim in their seasons."

Obviously, we are to see that a day was appointed as a holy convocation, a time of assembling together and resting. There was a day appointed by God, and seen as His feast. "Seven" in the scriptures is significant, for it speaks of completeness. There were seven days in the week, seven feasts of Jehovah, and all to be were to be observed in the first seven months of the Hebrew calendar. A sabbatical year was to be observed every seventh year, and upon completing seven times seven years, there was to be a year of Jubilee, or freedom.

Note, as well, that the Sabbath was not only to be a memorial throughout our generations, but it extended beyond public worship. This initial festival was to be a "...sabbath of the Lord in all your dwellings." We were to take it home and internalize its truth; to make it an intimate part of our life with God.

It is written that the Lord rested on the seventh day, and we memorialized that day which He appointed. When the Law was given on Sinai, these principles were established: "And Moses called all Israel, and said unto them, Hear, O Israel, the statutes and judgments which I speak in your ears this day, that ye may learn them, and keep, and do them. The Lord our God made a covenant with us in Horeb. The Lord made not this covenant with our fathers, but with us, even us, who are all of us here alive this day...Keep the sabbath day to sanctify it, as the Lord thy God hath commanded thee. Six days thou shalt labour, and do all thy work: But the seventh day is the sabbath of the Lord thy God: in it thou shalt not do any work, thou, nor thy son, nor thy daughter, nor thy manservant, nor thy maidservant, nor thine ox, nor thine ass, nor any of thy cattle, nor thy stranger that is within thy gates; that thy manservant and thy maidservant might rest as well as thou. And remember that thou wast a servant in the land of Egypt, and that the Lord thy God brought thee out thence through a mighty hand and by a stretched out arm: therefore the Lord thy God commanded thee to keep the sabbath day" (Deut. 5:1-3, 12-15).

Note that this day was not set apart for Israel alone, but for the manservants and maidservants, the cattle and the Gentiles who were part of the community. There was no time of rest in Egypt when Israel served in bondage, but now a permanent memorial was established so that God's people could enter His rest.

With the fall from grace and the consequence of sin came toil and labor; the sabbath pointed to a time when the curse would be removed and we would be redeemed. The coming of Messiah would usher in this rest.

Jesus, our Savior, was crucified on a Friday and rested in the earth on the Sabbath. He rose on Sunday, the first day of the week. He was the first begotten from the dead; the beginning of a new creation. In Jesus all things are new, and old things have passed away.

Eight numerically follows seven, and eight is of particular significance. On the eighth day of life the Hebrews were told to circumcise the male children. This was to be a physical or outward sign of an inward spiritual truth. It was a symbol of being separated unto God: a blood covenant, requiring the cutting of the flesh; literally, a *brit mi-lah*, or "covenant of cutting". Israel was instructed to circumcise the foreskin of the heart (Deut. 10:16) and pay homage to God.

Each firstborn male was to be offered up to God on the eighth day; the day that looked back toward the Law, and ahead to the start of a new dispensation or relationship. Thus a spiritual link was formed between the old and the new. With the completion or fulfillment of the former, our new hope begins by virtue of that which was finalized. *Shavuos*, or Pentecost, was observed on the fiftieth day, computing the completion of seven sabbaths (seven weeks from the Passover) and then culminating the eighth day, or the first day of the new week. This was to be the time when the Holy Spirit would be given to make us effective witnesses to the resurrection.

In referring to the Festival of *Succos* (Tabernacles, or Booths), we are enjoined by the word (Lev. 23:34-36): "Speak unto the children of Israel, saying, The fifteenth day of this seventh month shall be the feast of tabernacles for seven days unto the Lord. On the first day shall be an holy convocation: ye shall do no servile work therein. Seven days ye shall offer an offering made by fire unto the Lord: on the eighth day shall be an holy convocation unto you; and ye shall offer an offering made by fire unto the Lord: it is a solemn assembly; and ye shall do no servile work therein."

Here again we see that upon the completion of seven days, an eighth day was instituted as a time of holy convocation, and as a time of rest. Reference is made to this festival in the New Testament where it speaks of Jesus going to Jerusalem to observe this holy day (John 7:37): "In the last day, that great day of the feast..." *Sh'mini Atzeret*, or "the eighth day of assembly", was singled out for special honor, the eighth day referred to here as "the great day" of the feast. Once again the first day was a link to the previous seventh day of observance for this Levitical festival. We remain eminently aware of the past, but see the fulfillment or fruition in the Resurrection. We see a new start.

Precedent is clearly established, therefore, in recognizing the eighth day, or the first day of the new week, as a time of assembly, and honoring the new beginning. Following the crucifixion of Jesus, the disciples assembled on the first day of the week. Thomas (the doubting one) was absent that first Sunday, but we are told that on the following Sunday he was present (Jn. 20:26): "And after eight days again his disciples were within, and Thomas with them: then came Jesus, the doors being shut, and stood in the midst, and said, Peace be unto you (*Shalom aleichem*)."

This practice continued, frequently described as "the first day of the week": a time when they came to break bread, to engage in fellowship.

Paul, in writing to the congregation in Corinth, stated: "Upon the first day of the week, let every one of you lay by him in store, as God hath prospered him..." (1 Cor. 16:2). These faithful Jewish believers wanted to offer financial help to brothers and sisters in need, so Paul explained that when they came together on the first day to worship, it would be an appropriate time to take up a collection for the indigent. This was referred to, as well, as the Lord's Day.

Our unsaved Jewish brethren continue to worship on the seventh day; they remain under law, not recognizing the Resurrection and new life in Jesus. We, however, point beyond the law, satisfied by His blood atonement. Never losing our appreciation for the past and the law which brought us to faith, we nevertheless progress to our new beginning.

Leviticus 23 enjoins Israel to observe seven festivals, in addition to the Sabbath. These appointed holy days, as all the Law, are the shadows of things to come, pointing to Messiah. They have prophetic significance, some already fulfilled, and those which remain to come to realization in the future. The former include Passover, the Feast of Unleavened Bread, Firstfruits and Pentecost (*Shavuos*). Remaining to be fulfilled are the Feast of Trumpets, the Day of Atonement (*Yom Kippur*) and Tabernacles (*Succos*).

We saw that the Lord declared to Moses that he was to tell Israel about these festivals. Following the Sabbath were: "...the feasts of the Lord, even holy convocations, which ye shall proclaim in their seasons. In the fourteenth day of the first month at even is the Lord's passover" (Lev. 23:4-5).

Ex. 12:2-14 provides specific instructions for the observance of Passover. These regulations start with the announcement that this was to be considered the beginning of months, the first month of the new year. Our relationship with God begins at this point and is contingent upon understanding the spiritual significance of that which is to take place.

A lamb was to be selected for every family on the 10th of the month, and was to be held until the 14th. It was then to be slain, and the blood of the sacrificed lamb was to be applied to the doorposts and lintels of the homes. This blood was to be a token or sign for the *molech ha maves* (angel of death) to *pesach* (exempt or pass over) that home, while the firstborn in those homes not covered by the blood would be slain. Throughout the centuries the descendants of Israel conducted Passover *Seders* (the Hebrew word for "order" or "arrangement"), in commemoration of these events. A Passover *haggadah*, which includes many excerpts from the Exodus account, is distributed to each person in attendance. Complying with the instruction to narrate or tell it to all generations, we read the *haggadah*, literally, "the narration" or "the telling".

Most importantly, emphasis is made to create an awareness that each of us is to personally apply or internalize the events as if we were actually present. Failure to understand and make this application would render us unworthy to have been brought out of bondage.

What a glorious account is provided! We enter into the experience, beginning with the ritual of searching the home to make certain that every trace of *chometz*, or "leaven", has been removed. A *Seder* plate with symbolic elements is displayed to recapture the mindset of all who were captives in Egypt. Four cups of wine are consumed to remind us of the promises of God, and four questions (*kashers*) are asked to further ingrain how personal this experience was meant to be. With infinite care we re-enact a memorial service with precision; discussing, singing and reliving the time of our redemption. Passover is also known as *Chag Ha Matzot*, or "the Festival of *Matzah*" (unleavened bread). Upon leaving Egypt there was no time to allow the dough to rise, and we have unleavened bread to this day. Nothing with leaven is to be eaten for seven days. In preparation, therefore, homes are scrupulously cleaned to make certain that there is no leaven present. It is customary among the orthodox to light a candle to aid the search, to use a feather and spoon to gather every speck of dust from the corners of the rooms (lest there be any *chometz*), and to burn the leaven.

A *matzah tash*, usually a white linen bag with three compartments, is prominently displayed, and a slice of *matzah* is placed into each compartment. The middle *matzah* is broken in half: one half to be put back, and the other to be hidden, wrapped in a white linen napkin. Customarily, the children search for the hidden piece shortly before the end of the *Seder*. The one who finds the hidden *matzah* (*afikomen*) receives a prize.

The *Seder* plate includes *bitzah*, a hard-boiled egg, which reminds us of the freewill offering that was made when the Temple was standing. Parsley (*carpas*) reminds us that this is a spring festival, and also symbolizes the hyssop which was dipped into the blood and used to apply the token upon the homes that were to be spared. Bitter herbs, *moror* (horseradish), helps us to remember that our lives were made bitter in hard bondage and slavery. A mixture of apples, nuts and wine (*charoses*) is symbolic of the mortar used to build the pyramids with the labor of Hebrew slaves. A shankbone of a lamb (*z'roah*) is the symbol of the Passover, the lamb.

A special cup is placed on the table, called the "cup of Elijah". According to Malachi, he is to be the forerunner who announces the coming of Messiah. This portion of the service keeps us alert, looking for Elijah's coming. Customarily, someone is sent to open the door to see if Elijah, in fact, has arrived.

The four cups of wine of which we partake during the ceremony speak of four specific promises recorded in Exodus 6: "I will bring you out of bondage, I will redeem you with an outstretched arm, I will take you to me for a people and I will bring you into a land of promise".

The four questions, traditionally recited by the youngest male present, ask why this night is different from all other nights, and provides an opportunity to give the appropriate response to glorify God for our deliverance.

Prior to partaking of the *Seder* meal, there are special readings in the *haggadah*, ritual washings and blessings, eating portions of the *matzah* in the *tash* with bitter herbs and *charoses*, etc. The *matzah* and the events of the *Seder* speak most eloquently of Messiah:

1. *Matzah* is baked without leaven, the Biblical symbol of sin. Our Messiah was without sin.
2. *Matzah* is striped, which reminds us, as seen in Isaiah 53, "...with his stripes we are healed."
3. *Matzah* is pierced through with holes, and, according to Zechariah 12, we "...shall look upon me [him] whom they [we] have pierced..."

Three slices of *matzah* were placed inside the *tash*, for three speaks of the tri-unity of God: the Father, Son (Messiah) and Holy Spirit. There is but one *tash* hiding the three *matzot* inside, for the Trinity is veiled in a mystery; He is three-in-one. Admittedly, this contradicts normal Hebrew theology, but our fifth chapter dealt with the plurality of God in detail.

During the service a piece was broken from the middle *matzah* to be eaten with a piece from the upper *matzah* in the *tash*. Since Jesus is the only way to the Father, we must partake of Him to know God. One half of the middle *matzah* was left in the *tash*, for He was always part of the Godhead. Yet, one half was separated, for He became flesh to play a subordinate role for the purpose of redemption.

You will recall that one half was wrapped in a white linen napkin and was hidden. White linen symbolizes the burial of the righteous, and the hope of the resurrection. Customarily, that half, the *afikomen*, when found, is distributed to each person at the conclusion of the *Seder*. Nothing is eaten after this.

Chapter One described the two comings, so we need not repeat this. Note, however, that the prize of eternal life in Messiah is granted those who believe, and thus the one who discovers the buried or hidden *matzah* is rewarded. All who partake identify with Him, and are beneficiaries of this great hope. Since Jesus is our totality, nothing else is required. We say *"dei-einu"*, "it is sufficient".

It is customary to place the last piece of *matzah* from the *afikomen* on a high shelf, to be taken down the following year at the *Seder*. This, too, is a reminder that He is now seated at the right hand of the Father, but is coming back as outlined in our comments regarding Psalm 110.

Finally, it is important to note that *"afikomen"* is not Hebrew, but Greek. Literally, it speaks of something that was there, but is no longer in that place. It is understood as "He is risen", the reminder of the Resurrection from the dead.

The central figure of the *Seder* is the *Pesach*, the Passover, or lamb, which we are told to slay. Yes, kill the lamb and place the blood upon the doorposts and lintel of your home. We cannot overlook Lev. 17:11: "For the life of the flesh is in the blood: and I have given it to you upon the altar to make an atonement for your souls: for it is the blood that maketh an atonement for the soul."

The lamb was selected on the 10th day of Nisan and held for three days, to be slain on the 14th. Jesus was held for three days, fulfilling this same purpose. It was essential that the lamb be without spot or blemish, and our Passover Lamb was thus examined for three days and declared to be without sin. Trumped-up charges and lies were exposed by the declaration of Pilate: "...I find no fault in this man" (Luke 23:4).

It was customary to release a prisoner on Passover; the murderer Barabbas was set free, and the guiltless was sacrificed for our transgressions. This further testifies to Is. 53:4-5: "Surely he hath borne our griefs, and carried our sorrows: yet we did esteem him stricken, smitten of God, and afflicted. But he was wounded for our transgressions, he was bruised for our iniquities: the chastisement of our peace was upon him; and with his stripes, we are healed."

The lamb was held for three days and slain *bain ha arbayim*, or "between the evenings". Since the Temple days were divided into quarters, this would relate to between the sixth and ninth hours. Not only was Jesus crucified at this precise time, but it is recorded that there was darkness upon the face of the earth between the sixth and ninth hours. The Light of the world was snuffed out, and the consequence was total darkness, spiritual bankruptcy.

Since Jesus is our sin offering, as provided under law, we have been reconciled to a holy God. As the blood of the sacrificed lamb was a token of compliance, and demonstrated faith, so we are sanctified by His blood. Having been justified, we walk in the newness of life. Sin has no hold on those who are covered by the blood of Jesus. There is no need to crucify Him anew each time we sin (as was necessary with the animal sacrifice). When Jesus proclaimed on the tree "It is finished", He yielded up His spirit, and the requirement of the law was fulfilled.

The Feast of Unleavened Bread, then, is the walk of the one now justified by faith in His completed work. Our lives are to be sinless, without leaven present. His Word and Spirit are within us. As we give Him reign, totally yielded, He keeps us free to walk in the power of the resurrected life. Of special note is a promise that lends spiritual meaning to this truth: "For this commandment which I command thee this day, it is not hidden from thee, neither is it far off. It is not in heaven, that thou shouldest say, Who shall go up for us to heaven, and bring it unto us, that we may hear it, and do it? Neither is it beyond the sea, that thou shouldest say, Who shall go over the sea for us, and bring it unto us, that we may hear it, and do it? But the word is very nigh unto thee, in thy mouth, and in thy heart, that thou mayest do it" (Deut. 30:11-14).

The Living Word, Jesus, is in our hearts; we need not ascend to heaven or the depths of the earth to re-establish a relationship that is nigh (close). He has already paid the price of redemption, once and for all. We now can keep the Feast of Unleavened Bread.

Following the Feast of Unleavened Bread, according to Lev. 23:10-11, there is to be a sheaf of the firstfruit offering that is to be waved before the Lord. This offering is of all ripe fruits: grain, oil, wine, fleece, etc., and was to be free from blemish. Since the priests had no inheritance in Israel, they were to be given these offerings for their sustenance. Clearly, the first and the best belonged to God.

The pascal lamb was slain on the fourteenth, and the fifteenth (the Sabbath) was the beginning of Unleavened Bread. The following day, Sunday (the morrow after the Sabbath), or the first day of the week, was to be a firstfruit offering. Since Jesus rose on the first day of the week, the third day from the sacrifice of the lamb, He is the epitome of the firstfruit offering. He was without blemish or sin, in the prime of life, and the best that could be offered to God.

A second firstfruit offering was then to be made (Lev. 23:15-17, 20-21): "And ye shall count unto you from the morrow after the sabbath, from the day that ye brought the sheaf of the wave offering; seven sabbaths shall be complete: Even unto the morrow after the seventh sabbath shall ye number fifty days; and ye shall offer a new meat offering unto the Lord. Ye shall bring out of your habitations two wave loaves of two tenth deals: they shall be of fine flour; they shall be baken with leaven; they are the firstfruits unto the Lord...And the priest shall wave them with the bread of the firstfruits for a wave offering before the Lord, with the two lambs: they shall be holy to the Lord for the priest. And ye shall proclaim on the selfsame day, that it may be an holy convocation unto you: ye shall do no servile work therein: it shall be a statute for ever in all your dwellings throughout your generations."

Shavuos is the Hebrew for "weeks", which explains the name of the holiday. It is known also as *Chag Ha Katzir*, the "Feast of the Harvest", Pentecost (the Greek for "fiftieth"), and *Yom Ha Bikkurim*, the "Day of Firstfruits". It is associated as well with *Z'man mattan toraseinu*, or "the season of the giving of the *Torah*".

The day after Passover began the *sfira* days, or "days of counting". Seven sabbaths, or forty-nine days, were counted, and on the morrow, the fiftieth day, the harvest and offering were to take place. In contrast to the first *Bikkurim*, this offering was two wave loaves, both baked with leaven.

The initial offering from the barley harvest, which spoke of Jesus, paved the way for all. He rose on the third day, and we have that hope. The wheat harvest of the fiftieth day, with two waves loaves, represent the Jew and the Gentile. Although leaven is present (for all have sinned), the loaves are baked to show that the sin is purged.

It is recorded in Ex. 19:10-11 that the children of Israel were told to purify themselves for three days in preparation for the receiving of the *Torah* (Law). Thus, fifty days after leaving Egypt, the law was given on Sinai. Jewish people, unto this day, make this association.

On that day the trumpet sounded, fire appeared upon the mount, the wind roared and the ground quaked. All present trembled in the presence of an awesome God and His display of power. The voice of God was audible, and tradition teaches it was visible as well. According to the *Midrash*, or commentary, *"Sh'mos"* ("Names", the Hebrew term for the book of Exodus), all the nations on the face of the earth heard the commandments in their native language. The people saw a fiery substance, which was the manifestation of God's voice.

On Pentecost, according to the New Testament, Jews from all over the globe were in Jerusalem, since *Shavuos* is one of the *shlosh raglaim*, or "three pilgrimage festivals". All males were to come to Jerusalem on *Pesach, Shavuos* and *Succos* to appear before the Lord. On this day, following the Resurrection, there was a sound from heaven as a rushing and mighty wind. Cloven tongues of fire could be seen, and the Holy Spirit came to rest upon the people. Devout men of every nation were present, and all heard the disciples speak in their native tongues (Acts 2:1-6). It was understood that this not only paralleled the <u>first</u> *Shavuos*, but fulfilled the prophecy of Joel 2:28-32: "And it shall come to pass afterward, that I will pour out my spirit upon all flesh; and your sons and your daughters shall prophesy, your old men shall dream dreams, your young men shall see visions: And also upon the servants and upon the handmaids in those days will I pour out my spirit. And I will shew wonders in the heavens and in the earth, blood, and fire, and pillars of smoke. The sun shall be turned into darkness, and the moon into blood, before the great and the terrible day of the Lord come. And it shall come to pass, that whosoever shall call on the name of the Lord shall be delivered: for in mount Zion and in Jerusalem shall be deliverance, as the Lord hath said, and in the remnant whom the Lord shall call."

According to Deut. 29:14-15, it was declared that the covenant was made not only with those present, but "...also with him that is not here with us this day". The *Talmud* interprets this to mean all future generations of Jews, as well as future proselytes to the faith. Provision was always included for the Gentile to be part of the wave offering unto the Lord, for He has made, of two, one new creation.

It is customary for the Jewish people to eat dairy products during these days as a reminder that we were to be brought into a land of milk and honey. We also see this as a time to reflect on God's holy Law, and, in preparation, Orthodox Jews spend all night reading and studying *Torah*. Since life is held so precious, dairy, rather than flesh, is eaten, for none of God's creatures should be slain.

The *sfira* days were always days of joy in anticipation of the harvest and the commemoration of receiving the Law. However, this changed during the days of Rabbi Akiva, and we now view the *sfira* days as a time of reflection and mourning, leading up to a non-levitical (post-exilic) festival, *Lag B'Omer*.

During the Greco-Roman period, when Jerusalem was under

siege, no one could leave the city unless he was carried out in a coffin, feet first. As has been the case so many times in the history of Israel, great efforts were made to stop the effects of Judaism, which usually translated to killing the people, destroying their Temple, and, all-importantly, eliminating the *Torah*, the Word of their God.

To this day, burning synagogues and *Torahs* is the scheme of the devil to thwart the Jew from bringing the Word to the nations. In so doing, the will of God, and the passion the Jew has for preserving this truth, is overlooked. In any event, one more time the insidious plan of Satan was in progress, and one more time, God's chosen people rose to the occasion.

The great rabbi of the day, Yochanan ben Zaccai, was determined to preserve the *Torah* as the means to educate his people. Feigning death, he was carried out in a coffin, and escaped to Yavneh, where he established an academy or *yeshiva*, to train Jews in the ways of the *Torah*.

The great general Vespasian approached, and Yochanan went out to greet him in his most ornate regalia. He addressed Vespasian as "Emperor", which was taken as a sign by the general, who had had a vision of a holy man in ornate garb, and received Yochanan with respect. Since Yochanan had a reputation as a man of peace, he was allowed to practice his faith, and train his pupils. It was shortly thereafter that the emperor died, and Vespasian succeeded him.

After the death of Yochanan ben Zaccai, the *nasi*, or "president", of the *yeshiva* was Rabbi Gamliel. He continued the teaching of the students, and the preservation of the *Torah*. During this period the *Beth Din*, or Jewish high court, was re-established, as were the basis for the calendar (setting dates by the lighting of bonfires at the sighting of the new moon), and codification of the law, which laid the foundation for the *mishnah*.

There were two schools of thought regarding *Torah* which prevailed: that of Shammai and that of Hillel. Shammai was stringent, and Hillel more benevolent. The teaching of Hillel which best typifies his approach to God is a story of a proselyte who asked to be taught the principles of *Torah "al regel achat"*, "while standing on one foot", or "quickly". Hillel's response was, "Thou shalt love the Lord thy God with all thy heart, with all thy strength and with all thy might. And thou shalt love thy neighbor as thyself." Hillel declared that all else is commentary.

The codification of the law was intended to unite the schools of Hillel and Shammai. It resulted in publishing a *siddur*, or prayer book, whereby a pattern of prayer was established. This was viewed as a means through which controversy would be eliminated. Certainly the desire was genuine and well-intended, but it lead to ritualism and did not leave room for the Holy Spirit.

Perhaps the greatest and best-known rabbi succeeded Gamliel, and that was Rabbi Akiva. He was a poor shepherd who was an illiterate until the age of forty. Akiva tended the sheep of a rich man by the name of Kalba Shavua, and fell in love with his daughter, Rachel. Rachel loved Akiva, and recognized his potential. She agreed to marry him with the proviso that he would become educated in *Torah*. Overwhelmed by the prospect of gaining an education at such an advanced age, Akiva sat by a stream with his sheep and pondered the matter.

As he sat there, his attention was drawn to a great boulder that had a hole in its middle. He wondered what could possibly have penetrated such a hard and seemingly impenetrable object. Then he saw a drop of water fall into the center of the rock, and he realized that, over the course of time, the water wore its way through. He took this as a sign from God. If something as soft as water could penetrate a rock, the Word of God would be able to enter his skull.

At the age of forty, Akiva began his education, and went on to become one of the greatest *Torah* scholars in Jewish history. His fame spread throughout the world, and he traveled all over, not only teaching students, but teaching teachers how to teach. It is said that Akiva had over 24,000 *talmidim*, or pupils, and was greatly instrumental in preserving *Torah*. He is revered by the Jewish people, and regarded as one of the most influential and important instrumentalities of God.

This brings us to the subject at hand. During the *sfira* days (the days of the counting of the *omer*), a plague broke out and 24,000 pupils of Rabbi Akiva lost their lives. The *sfira* days are the days of counting from the day after Passover until *Shavuos*. The Hebrew word *lispor*, or "to count", stems from the Levitical commandment to count seven Sabbaths to *Shavuos*, which would be observed on the fiftieth day. The precious Word of God was in jeopardy, for the students of Akiva were practically wiped out. However, on the thirty-third day of the counting of the *omer* (the dry measure for the offering of the harvest), the plague suddenly stopped.

The Hebrew letter *lamed*, or "L", has a numerical equivalent of 30, and the letter *gimmel*, or "G", is 3. Thus, *Lag* is the Hebrew that points us to the thirty-third day of the counting of the *omer*, leading up to the fiftieth day, *Shavuos*. To the present, the 33rd day is a time of remembrance and rejoicing for the Jewish people. The plague was stopped, and the precious Word of God was preserved. We regard *Lag B'Omer* as a scholar's holiday, and praise God for the Jewish lives that kept the *Torah* alive.

When Jews enter a home or synagogue, they touch the *mezuzah* on the doorpost, and kiss their fingers in deference to the Word of God. There is a great reverence and respect for the Word, and believers could learn a lot from Jewish people when it comes to respect for the Word.

In the synagogue, the *Torah* scrolls are housed in an ark behind a veil. When the curtains are drawn back, the congregants rise out of respect for the Word. Those who are called up for an *aliyah*, or pilgrimage, go up to the *bema*, or dais, to recite the traditional blessings, touch the *Torah* with the *tzitzit*, or fringes, of the *tallis*, or prayer shawl, and then kiss the fringes and touch the place from which the portion of the *Torah* is to be read. Upon finishing the reading of the *Torah*, the scroll is carried around the synagogue, and the congregants (males wearing the prayer shawls) touch the *Torah* and kiss the *tzitzit* in deference for the sacred Word. Women in the congregation similarly kiss the *Torah*. What a tribute to the Jewish mindset in their deep abiding awe of *Torah*!

The scrolls of the *Torah* are wound around wooden poles, and these poles or sticks are referred to as *Etz Chai*, the "tree of life". It is an honor, indeed, for the Jew to come in contact with the sacred Word that imparts life.

Lag B'Omer is not one of the Levitical festivals, but it is an important reminder of how the Jew views his *Torah*. We thank God for the faithfulness of the Yochanan ben Zaccais, the Gamliels and Akivas who put life and limb on the line so that we could have the *Torah* we enjoy to this day. Akiva was flayed alive with burning coals, but in his dying breath paid tribute to God. Many like him died *al kiddush ha shem*, or "for the sanctity of the name of God". *Lag B'Omer* is a precious reminder of the debt of gratitude we owe to the Jewish people for preserving the *Torah* (scripture), which has remained intact to this day.

The Jewish people have a reputation for being a stubborn nation. Not only have they not cornered the market on stubbornness, but this attribute helped them to remain steadfast in spite of every obstacle. Keeping the tradition and teaching of *Torah* flourishing is the legacy resulting from such determination.

On *Shavuos*, the book of Ruth is read in the synagogue. Naomi had lost her husband and two sons, and famine prevailed in the land of Israel. She decided to return to her country and told her two daughters-in-law to go back to their country, Moab. One daughter-in-law, Orpah, relented and went back to her kindred, but the other, Ruth, refused to leave. As much as Naomi pleaded, she could not convince Ruth to leave. Ruth is a beautiful example of the Gentile who embraces the God of Israel and His people. Ruth went out into the fields, at her mother-in-law's direction, to glean wheat during the harvest. She gleaned in the fields of Boaz, a near-kinsman according to the flesh. Boaz, whose name means "strength", is a picture of the *goel*, or kinsman-redeemer, which was provided under the law. He had the right of redemption, and the right to raise up seed unto the deceased. The progeny of Ruth and Boaz was Obed, the father of Jesse, the father of David. So Ruth was to be included in the lineage of Messiah.

The book preceding the book of Ruth is Judges. This book ends with the comment: "In those days there was no king in Israel: every man did that which was right in his own eyes" (21:25). There was a famine in the land of Israel, which had caused Naomi and her husband, Elimelech, to go to Moab. However, there was also a famine of the Word, for that is why all did as they thought appropriate in their own eyes. There continues to be a famine of the hearing of the Word, and our people continue to do what they deem right, rather than abide by the Word.

It is interesting to note that under Levitical law, the harvester was enjoined not to glean the corners of the field, but to leave them for the needy and the stranger. Provision was made in God's law for Ruth, the alien to the commonwealth of Israel. If that were not enough, the servants of Boaz were told not only to allow Ruth to glean the corners, but they were to leave handfuls, on purpose!

God continues to leave handfuls on purpose, for it is His desire that both Jew and Gentile be fed the Word. It is by the hearing of the Word we come to faith. *Shavuos*, then, produces the desired harvest of Jew and Gentile, the two wave loaves.

The husband of Naomi is named "Elimelech", a compound of two Hebrew words, "God" and "King". Our God and King desires all to be part of the harvest, and He makes adequate provision. When Ruth and Naomi returned to the ancestral home of David, Bethlehem, the redeemer (Boaz) was there. He is described as a mighty man of wealth. Our Redeemer certainly matches that description, and He will provide all our needs according to His riches in glory. He, too, came from Bethlehem or *Bet Lechem*, the "house of bread", so we shall never hunger.

Passover (*Pesach*), Unleavened Bread (*Matzot*) and Pentecost (*Shavuos*) are spring festivals which have been spiritually fulfilled. They speak of the freedom from bondage or sin and being covered by the blood of the Lamb (Passover); the walk of the believer (Unleavened Bread); Messiah the firstfruit offering, and the harvest of souls for both Jew and Gentile (Shavuos).

A hiatus follows, during which time it would seem that nothing is happening. To some extent, this is what appears to be taking place today. Although two thousand years have elapsed, the Lord is far from through with completing His program. Jewish people do not recognize the coming of Messiah in His first appearance, and nominal Christians say, "Where is the promise of His coming?" (2 Peter 3:4).

"The time(s) of the Gentiles" (Luke 21:24) remains to be fulfilled, but make no mistake, Jesus is coming back! No man knows the day or the hour, in spite of all the books and treatises that have been written on this subject. We do know, however, that the Levitical festivals which are to take place in the latter part of the year provide insight in this regard.

Things will happen with great rapidity, and all within the seventh month of the Hebrew calendar (the number of completion). It begins with what the scriptures refer to as *Yom Teruah*, "The Day of the Sounding of the Alarm", or "Trumpets". This solemn period is more commonly known as *Rosh Ha Shanna*, or the "New Year".

The Biblical foundation is laid in Lev. 23:23-25: "And the Lord spake unto Moses, saying, Speak unto the children of Israel, saying, In the seventh month, in the first day of the month, shall ye have a sabbath, a memorial of blowing of trumpets, an holy convocation. Ye shall do no servile work therein: but ye shall offer an offering made by fire unto the Lord."

A *shofar*, or ram's horn, is blown at the sighting of each new moon, or month. This, then, is the seventh trumpet, and it alerts us to the beginning of the second and final half of God's program: He is now to resume dealing with Israel. The elect had been set aside in order to bring the Gentiles to salvation, but now the clock starts to tick again. The seventieth week of Daniel's prophecy remains to be fulfilled.

In Jewish circles we begin to prepare for a new year. Cards and greetings declare *L'shanna tovah tikateivu*, "For a good year may you be written down", or "inscribed". The hope is for one to be recorded in the Book of Life. *Nisan*, the month of the Passover, was declared to be the first month of the year, and *Tishrei* is the seventh. Jewish people customarily distinguish between the civil and the religious years. Tradition teaches this is the anniversary of creation, and it is known too as *Yom Hazikaron*, "the Day of Remembrance". The blowing of the *shofar* is a spiritual wake-up call for Israel.

The commentary on *t'shuveh*, or repentance, brings a warning: "Awake, ye sleepers, from your sleep...ponder over your deeds; remember your Creator and go back to Him in penitence. Be not of those seeking after vain things which cannot profit or deliver. Look well to your improper thoughts and return to God so that He may have mercy upon you."

We refer to the ten-day period leading up to *Yom Kippur* (the Day of Atonement, which is the next Levitical festival) as *Yamim Nora'im*, the "Days of Awe". Our rabbis tell us that we pass before our Creator as sheep before a shepherd, and our fate is to be decided upon the Day of Atonement. The righteous have been inscribed in the Book of Life, but those whose deeds are wanting, or the "borderline cases", have a ten-day respite to balance the scales in their favor. Upon the completion of the ten days they are either worthy to be recorded in the Book of Life, or they are destined for destruction. Although the Word of God teaches "...the just shall live by his faith" (Hab. 2:4), the concept of *mitzvot*, or "good deeds", still prevails. As God resumes His dealing with Israel, the trumpet sounds. We are grateful that Zechariah prophesied that the spirit of grace and supplication will be poured out upon the house of Israel and the house of Judah, and that we will look upon Him Whom we have pierced. This is a message for our Jewish brethren so that they will respond to the trumpet's call.

Continuing in Lev. 23:26-29: "And the Lord spake unto Moses, saying, Also on the tenth day of this seventh month there shall be a day of atonement: it shall be an holy convocation unto you; and ye shall afflict your souls, and offer an offering made by fire unto the Lord. And ye shall do no work in that same day: for it is a day of atonement, to make an atonement for you before the Lord your God. For whatsoever soul it be that shall not be afflicted in that same day, he shall be cut off from among his people."

On the first day of *Tishrei* the trumpet blared, announcing a call to judgment; now, on the tenth, another holy convocation, and a time to afflict the soul. Israel had to come to repentance, to return to God. This necessitated a serious appraisal of the attitude of the heart. Numbers 29 and the book of Exodus add that one kid of the goats for a sin offering of atonement was required. The blood upon the altar was provision for the *kippora*, or "covering", for sin.

Modern Judaism, with the destruction of the Temple, views prayer as the atonement. In fact, a prayer is recited in which we profess that we fast to diminish our blood in place of the blood shed upon the altar, for we no longer have the atonement provided according to the law. The object lesson of God, however, is hard to overlook. Mercy is extended to those who, by faith, accept the completed work of Jesus on the tree. His righteousness is then ours by imputation.

Let us remember the words of Hosea (14:1-4): "O Israel, return unto the Lord thy God; for thou hast fallen by thine iniquity. Take with you words, and turn to the Lord: say unto Him, Take away all iniquity, and receive us graciously: so we will render the calves of our lips. Asshur shall not save us; we will not ride upon horses: neither will we say any more to the work of our hands, Ye are our gods: for in thee the fatherless findeth mercy. I will heal their backsliding, I will love them freely: for mine anger is turned away from him."

It is argued that we take words in prayer which satisfy as the atonement, but that is a poor rendering of the truth seen here. *Teshuveh*, or "repentance", requires confession, and we are to understand that our words are agreement that we are sinners, and He has the right to judge us guilty under law.

It is God who must take away our iniquity, and that graciously, or by unmerited favor. God's grace and forgiveness is not the result of our *mitzvot*, or "good deeds", but His mercy. The "calves of our lips" are the penitent confession and humbled spirit. They replace the calves that were offered while the altar stood in Jerusalem.

Asshur (Assyria), or any nation for that matter, is not the answer. No alliance with the powers of the world are of any consequence. It certainly is not the "work of our hands". God alone can heal our backsliding and remove His righteous anger, when we come on His terms. David said it quite clearly in Ps. 32:1-2: "Blessed is he whose transgression is forgiven, whose sin is covered. Blessed is the man unto whom the Lord imputeth not iniquity, and in whose spirit there is no guile." Likewise, this same plea is reiterated by David, revealing the need for God to provide the acceptable atonement: "Have mercy upon me, O God, according to thy lovingkindness: according unto the multitude of thy tender mercies blot out my transgressions. Wash me throughly from mine iniquity, and cleanse me from my sin. For I acknowledge my transgressions; and my sin is ever before me" (Ps. 51:1-3).

Perhaps with this in view we can now see that sacrifice, without repentance, is of no consequence. Verses 15-17 and 19 of this psalm foster this realization: "O Lord, open thou my lips, and my mouth shall shew forth thy praise. For thou desirest not sacrifice; else would I give it: thou delightest not in burnt offering. The sacrifices of God are a broken spirit: a broken and contrite heart, O God, thou wilt not despise...Then shalt thou be pleased with the sacrifices of righteousness, with burnt offering and whole burnt offering: then shall they offer bullocks upon thine altar."

Only when our attitude is right are our ritual sacrifices acceptable. Prayer and fasting, as are presently practiced on *Yom Kippor*, is not the answer. This too is clear from the Word of God: "Cry aloud, spare not, lift up the voice like a trumpet, and shew my people their transgression, and the house of Jacob their sins. Yet they seek me daily, and delight to know my ways, as a nation that did righteousness, and forsook not the ordinance of their God: they ask of me the ordinances of justice; they take delight in approaching to God. Wherefore have we fasted, say they, and thou seest not? wherefore have we afflicted our soul, and thou takest no knowledge?" (Is. 58:1-3).

Fasting has become an act of righteousness. We expect to receive forgiveness because of our deeds. God never owes us, or is in any way obligated, to forgive. His mercy endures forever, but depends upon our recognizing that He delights in forgiving those who do not deserve forgiveness. We must confess and turn from the sin.

Isaiah continues to show Israel the error of such thinking (vs. 4-5): "Behold, ye fast for strife and debate, and to smite with the fist of wickedness: ye shall not fast as ye do this day, to make your voice to be heard on high. Is it such a fast that I have chosen? a day for man to afflict his soul? is it to bow down his head as a bulrush, and to spread sackcloth and ashes under him? wilt thou call this a fast, and an acceptable day to the Lord?"

We become martyrs in our minds, depriving ourselves of food, and become testy and contentious. This is not what the Lord desires, and in no way satisfies the "affliction" of the soul. We have no voice to raise to God in justification, but can only humbly beg forgiveness, and live from that point forward with a hunger and thirst for His righteousness. The promise, as ever, is: "Then shalt thou delight thyself in the Lord; and I will cause thee to ride upon the high places of the earth, and feed thee with the heritage of Jacob thy father: for the mouth of the Lord hath spoken it" (v. 14).

Yes, we will mourn for Him as one mourns for his only son, and shall be in bitterness for Him as one who is in bitterness for his firstborn. He alone can provide the new heart and new spirit which empower us to continue in His word. We must come to realize that *Yom Kippor* is the Day of Calvary, and His death upon the tree is the only act acceptable to God the Father.

Another portion of the scriptures read in the synagogue on *Yom*

Kippor is the book of Jonah. Most are somewhat familiar with this account of the prophet being swallowed by a great fish (not necessarily a whale). Jonah was told to go to Nineveh to warn the people to repent, for God's judgment upon them was imminent. Jonah chose to run, rather than accede to the will of God. Many imagine that Jonah deemed it impossible for such a sinful people to turn from their sin, and that is why he chose to disobey. However, the reason is revealed in Jonah 4:2: "And he prayed unto the Lord, and said, I pray thee, O Lord, was not this my saying, when I was in my country? Therefore I fled before unto Tarshish: for I knew that thou art a gracious God, and merciful, slow to anger, and of great kindness, and repentest thee of evil."

Jonah had judged the people unworthy of God's grace, and ran away. He defied God, but was given a second opportunity to comply. Although he did the Lord's bidding the second time, he still did not learn his lesson. God had to deal with him further.

Jonah sat under a gourd that God had prepared for him as protection from the sun. God then caused a worm to smite the gourd which caused it to wither, so that the sun bore down upon Jonah without mercy. Jonah wished at this point that he would die. This prompted God to question Jonah: "...Doest thou well to be angry for the gourd?...Then said the Lord, thou hast had pity on the gourd, for the which thou hast not laboured, neither madest it grow; which came up in a night, and perished in a night: And should not I spare Nineveh, that great city, wherein are more than sixscore thousand persons that cannot discern between their right hand and their left hand; and also much cattle?" (vs. 9-11).

Hopefully, we all can learn this *Yom Kippor* lesson as did Jonah. God will have mercy upon whom He will, and we are not to judge in our hearts. *Yom Kippor* is the time to receive the unmerited favor of God, but can we receive forgiveness and not offer forgiveness ourselves?

Nineveh was described as exceedingly wicked, yet, upon the hearing of the Word proclaimed by Jonah, the cry went out to turn from their evil ways. A fast was proclaimed, and the people repented in sackcloth and ashes, a sign of deep humility. For they inquired (3:9): "Who can tell if God will turn and repent, and turn away from his fierce anger, that we perish not?" None to this day can answer that question, but we must act in obedience to His will. We must forgive as we are forgiven, and allow God to work His sovereign will to His honor and glory.

Many have judged Israel unworthy, and have not brought the gospel to those who are called the "elect of God". Yet the scriptures teach that the gospel is "to the Jew first" (Romans 1:16). Our prayer is that with a heightened awareness of the role played by the Jew, more people will bring this message of hope and forgiveness.

The final Levitical festival takes place on the fifteenth of *Tishrei*. "And the Lord spake unto Moses, saying, Speak unto the children of Israel, saying, The fifteenth day of this seventh month shall be the feast of tabernacles for seven days unto the Lord. On the first day shall be an holy convocation: ye shall do no servile work therein. Seven days ye shall offer an offering made by fire unto the Lord: on the eighth day shall be an holy convocation unto you; and ye shall offer an offering made by fire unto the Lord: it is a solemn assembly; and ye shall do no servile work therein" (Lev. 23:33-36). Subsequent verses explain how this festival derives its name (vs. 39-43): "Also in the fifteenth day of the seventh month, when ye have gathered in the fruit of the land, ye shall keep a feast unto the Lord seven days: on the first day shall be a sabbath, and on the eighth day shall be a sabbath. And ye shall take you on the first day the boughs of goodly trees, branches of palm trees, and the boughs of thick trees, and willows of the brook; and ye shall rejoice before the Lord your God seven days. And ye shall keep it a feast unto the Lord seven days in the year. It shall be a statute for ever in your generations: ye shall celebrate it in the seventh month. Ye shall dwell in booths seven days; all that are Israelites born shall dwell in booths: That your generations may know that I made the children of Israel to dwell in booths, when I brought them out of the land of Egypt: I am the

Lord your God."

Chag Succos is the Festival of Booths, or Tabernacles, since frail huts were to be built as temporary dwellings. They are a reminder of the booths used by the children of Israel during the forty years in the wilderness. Whereas the *succah* is fragile, it emphasizes that our faith is in God, Who alone is our security. In fact, the roof was constructed of branches in such a way that the sky and stars could be seen. Our eyes are to be heavenward, and we are to remain aware that He is our covering.

Included in the observance is the use of four species: a citron (*esrog*); a palm branch (*lulav*); a myrtle branch (*hadas*); and a willow branch (*arava*). The branches are held together and are called the *lulav*, which is the largest of the species. We are to love the Lord, our God, with all our heart, our soul and our strength. The *lulav* symbolizes the spinal cord, or physical man, who bows to the Lord, and the citron (a lemon-like fruit) epitomizes the heart.

While the Temple stood, a joyous ceremony, or water libation, roused a deep sense of the presence of the Holy Spirit. A procession known as *Simchat bet ha sho-evah*, the joyous "ceremony of the water-drawing", highlighted this spiritual closeness. The priests drew water from the pool of Siloam as an offering to the Lord. Isaiah 55 extends an invitation for all who are thirsty to come and drink without money or price. He reminds us that we labor for that which brings no satisfaction, but if we hearken diligently, God will satisfy the soul. He will make an everlasting covenant, even the sure mercies of David.

Water is the symbol of the Holy Spirit, and the free gift of God. No price can be offered, for once again we are reminded that we can only accept what He offers. Actually, there is a price, but He paid it.

In the New Testament, in John 7, we read that it was the Feast of Tabernacles and the Jewish people flowed into Jerusalem. It is significant to note what took place: "In the last day, that great day of the feast, Jesus stood and cried, saying, If any man thirst, let him come unto me, and drink. He that believeth on me, as the scripture hath said, out of his belly shall flow rivers of living water" (Jn. 7:37-38). As the priests were carrying the pitchers of water from the pool of Siloam, Israel's Messiah used the occasion to bring out the spiritual message, as did Isaiah. It was the last day, known as *Hoshanna Rabbah*, "the great salvation". Come unto Him and receive the Spirit; enter into the *Brit Olam*, the "everlasting covenant" of David.

During the recitation of the *Hallel* from the Psalms (113-118), as was customary, a prayer for salvation was uttered: "I will praise Thee: for Thou hast heard me, and art become my salvation. The stone which the builders refused [rejected] is become the head stone of the corner. This is the Lord's doing; it is marvellous in our eyes. This is the day which the Lord hath made; we will rejoice and be glad in it. Save now, I beseech Thee, O Lord: O Lord, I beseech Thee, send now prosperity. Blessed be he that cometh in the name of the Lord: we have blessed you out of the house of the Lord" (Ps. 118:21-26). The next verses have deep meaning for us as well: "God is the Lord, which hath shewed us light: bind the sacrifice with cords, even unto the horns of the altar. Thou art my God, and I will praise thee: thou art my God, I will exalt thee" (vs. 27-28).

In the seventh month, the final stage of God's program, before it is too late, another attempt is made to open our eyes. Come to Jesus for living water, the great salvation. Come to Jesus, Who was the Rejected One, and receive satisfaction without price. Come and see the One Who was bound to the altar, the sacrificed Lamb Who takes away the sin of the world.

Jeremiah gave a very stern warning (2:12-13): "Be astonished, O ye heavens, at this, and be horribly afraid, be ye very desolate, saith the Lord. For my people have committed two evils; they have forsaken me the fountain of living waters, and hewed out cisterns, broken cisterns, that can hold no water." Before it is too late, the invitation is given to come to the fount, the Source of life. Broken or sinful lives cannot house the Spirit of God, and without His righteousness there is no hope. He promises a new heart and new spirit.

Be horribly afraid to allow another day to pass in disobedience or rejection of His gracious offer.

After seven days in the *succah*, an eighth day of holy convocation is to take place. This is the conclusion festival called *Shmini Atzeret*, the "eighth day of assembly". Eight, you will recall, speaks of the new beginning, looking ahead, and links to the law, looking back. The rabbis tell us that it is so difficult for our Lord to part company with us, that after the completion of the seven-day festival, an eighth day is added for additional enjoyment.

On *Shmini Atzeret* the Jewish worshippers complete the annual cycle of the reading of the *Torah*, so we call the second day of the conclusion festival *Simchat Torah*, or "Rejoicing in the *Torah*". It is marked by seven processions around the synagogue carrying all the *Torah* scrolls. Joy prevails as the people dance and sing, and even the children are encouraged to participate. We are reminded of Paul's comment that his people "...have a zeal of God, but not according to knowledge" (Romans 10:2). Messiah is the end of the law for righteousness unto everyone who believes. All are condemned by the perfection of the Law we could never keep. Jesus, born of a virgin, without sin, fulfilled that law so that we could come to God through Him. All the Levitical festivals point to this great truth.

God's desire had always been to have fellowship with man, the crowning glory of His creation. Genesis records that the Lord walked with Adam and Eve in the garden of Eden. This relationship was destroyed by sin. However, the wilderness Tabernacle, the representation of God's presence on earth, was with Israel. Our sages tell us that the *succah* is reminiscent of the Tabernacle, and God dwelling with man. Thus, *Succos* is, all importantly, a prophetic indication of the fellowship that will be restored between God and man. The Hebrew word for tabernacle, *mishkan*, is from the root "to dwell" or "abide", and so our Lord will tabernacle with His people.

David made preparation for the construction of the Temple, which was to become the symbolic dwelling place of God upon the earth. Solomon (*Shlomo*, or "peace") completed and dedicated the

Temple because David had blood on his hands. That Temple was ultimately destroyed, and Israel and Judah were carried into captivity.

In the books of Ezra, Nehemiah and Zechariah we find a lot of detail regarding the reconstruction of the Temple, when the Jews returned from Babylon. Portions of Zechariah are read during *Chanukah*, the Feast of the Dedication. This is an eight-day festival known also as the Festival of Lights. Although *Chanukah* is not a Levitical festival, it is Biblically oriented, and an important part of Jewish history. It lends further import to the Jewish mindset and heart regarding God's presence in the Temple and the reverence for *Torah*.

We read this promise in Zech. 2:10-11: "Sing and rejoice, O daughter of Zion: for, lo, I come, and I will dwell in the midst of thee, saith the Lord. And many nations shall be joined to the Lord in that day, and shall be my people: and I will dwell in the midst of thee, and thou shall know that the Lord of hosts hath sent me unto thee."

Whereas rabbinical commentary tends to depersonalize and play down these words, the Lord's stated intention is to dwell in our midst. God the Father, the Lord of hosts, will send Jesus in fulfillment of this promise. According to verse 13: "Be silent, O all flesh, before the Lord: for He is raised up out of His holy habitation."

Yes, be still, for God has left the habitation of heaven to reveal Himself to us in the person of Jesus. He has taken residence in the hearts of His people, in His first coming, and He will be back to dwell in our midst.

Chapter 3 of Zechariah reveals a vision of Joshua the high priest, and Satan resisting him. Although Joshua is clothed in filthy garments, the Lord says: "...I have caused thine iniquity to pass from thee, and I will clothe thee with a change of raiment" (v. 4). Our filth or sin has been removed, and we have been clothed in the imputed righteousness of Jesus. It is the Lord Who resists Satan, and we can now enjoy a relationship in His presence as a result.

In another vision recorded in Zechariah 4, our attention is drawn to a *menorah*, or candelabra, which represents the light of God, and His plan to restore the Temple. We must recognize, however, per verse 6: "...This is the word of the Lord unto Zerubbabel, saying, Not by might, nor by power, but by my spirit, saith the Lord of hosts." As the oil in the *menorah* is the unseen source of power that keeps the flame alive, God is the unseen source of all light that dispels the darkness of sin. It is not our deeds or strength, but His.

We are told that when the Maccabees rededicated the Temple in 165 BCE, which had been defiled, there was but a single cruse of the sacred oil, which was enough to last but one day. It would take eight days to prepare the necessary oil to make certain that the eternal flame would not be extinguished. God performed a miracle in allowing the single cruse to last the eight-day period, and we celebrate eight days of *Chanukah* as a memorial.

There are other non-Levitical festivals which are observed by the Jewish people. Mention was made of *Purim* in a previous chapter. This is the Hebrew word for "lots", which was the means by which a date had been established for the annihilation of the Jews. God turned the tables on wicked Haman, and *Purim* became a joyous festival recalling the redemption of the nation. It is a festive time for *shalach monos*, or the "sending of portions". On the 13th of the Hebrew month *Adar*, it is customary to fast. *Tanas Esther*, or the "Fast of Esther", commemorates the request of Esther that the people fast and plead that God would spare her, in bringing her petition to deliver the nation, before the king. The following day, the 14th of *Adar*, is the celebration of *Purim*, marked by the reading of the book of Esther, wearing costumes and having parades. In the reading of the *megillas Esther*, *groggers*, or noisemakers, are used to drown out the name of Haman, the descendant of Agag, and the symbol of anti-semitic activity throughout the generations. Haman, of course, along with his ten sons, was hung from the very gallows built to execute Mordecai.

All importantly, we remember that although the name of God

does not appear in the story of Esther, His hand can be seen at every turn by enlightened people. He orchestrated all these events, keeping His promise that "No weapon that is formed against thee shall prosper..." (Is. 54:17). As the name "Esther" has the root *sater*, or "hidden", we learn to search out the hidden things of God. Isaiah 48:6 best sums this up: "...I have shewed thee new things from this time, even hidden things, and thou didst not know them."

Haman in the Hebrew means "clamor". He indeed caused an uproar and raised his voice against God's people. He paid the price for going against the will of the Lord. Esther *bas Avi Chayil* (the daughter of the Father of Might) was sent by God to turn the tide. We remember, too, that the name of the king of the realm, Ahasuerus, is a compound of the Hebrew *achar* (last) and *reishis* (first). He is the first and the last, the alpha and the omega. Once again, concealed in a mystery, it is the hand of God which brings victory.

The saddest and most tragic day of the Hebrew calendar is known as *Tisha B'Av*, or the "ninth of *Av*". It is a day of fasting and mourning which commemorates the destruction of Solomon's Temple in 586 BCE, and also of the reconstructed Temple, which was destroyed on this same date in 70 CE.

Other tragic events on this date include the expulsion of the Jews from Spain in 1492, and the Jewish villages in Poland which were wiped out during the Holocaust. Tradition teaches, as well, that it was on *Tisha B'Av* that the ten spies, sent by Joshua to survey the land of Canaan, came back with their evil report. Actually, the mourning period starts with the 17th of *Tammuz*, three weeks earlier, for this is the date that the city walls were breached, leading to the destruction of Jerusalem.

In the synagogue we read the scripture portion from Exodus 32 dealing with the sin of the golden calf. Moses ascended the mount to receive God's Law, and was to be gone forty days and nights. His return was anticipated on the 16th of *Tammuz*, but the fortieth day was actually the 17th. The people lost heart, and asked for a representation of God that could be seen and worshipped. Thus, the golden calf was fashioned by the hands of man. The lesson is clear: we are to follow God's timetable, and not man's. We wait upon the Lord, abide faithful, and never trust the work of our hands.

Other fast days include the 10th of *Tevat*, which marks the beginning of the siege of Jerusalem, and the Fast of Gedaliah on the 3rd of *Tishrei*, the day after *Rosh Ha Shannah*. Gedaliah was appointed as governor by Nebuchadnezzer at the time of the Babylonian captivity, and was executed in an evil plot by his countrymen.

Days of joy established in the post-exilic period include *Yom Ha Atzmaut* and *Yom Yerushalayim*. The former is Israel's Independence Day, celebrated on the 5th of *Iyar*, marking the establishment of the Jewish state in 1948. On the 28th of *Iyar*, we commemorate Jerusalem Day, which was the date in 1967 when we saw the reunification of this ancestral city of Judaism. For the first time since 70 CE, the ancient parts of the city, including the Western Wall (Wailing Wall) and the Temple mount, were restored to Jewish sovereignty.

This is the only city in all the Word of God for which we are enjoined to offer prayer. We are not to forget, as well, per Psalm 122, "...they shall prosper that love thee."

10

THE TIME OF JACOB'S TROUBLE

We mentioned that the period preceding the return of Messiah is called the Great Tribulation, or the Time of Jacob's Trouble. Historically, the Lord always reaches a point in which action must be taken against sin. This was demonstrated with the flood in Noah's day, the destruction of Sodom and Gomorrah in Abraham's day, and even with the judgment upon the Temple and Jerusalem. Israel's prophets warn of this impending calamity yet to take place: "For the day of the Lord of hosts shall be upon every one that is proud and lofty, and upon every one that is lifted up; and he shall be brought low...And the loftiness of man shall be bowed down, and the haughtiness of men shall be made low: and the Lord alone shall be exalted in that day...And they shall go into the holes of the rocks, and into the caves of the earth, for fear of the Lord, and for the glory of his majesty, when he ariseth to shake terribly the earth" (Is. 2:12, 17, 19). Isaiah continues this theme in chapter 13: "Howl ye; for the day of the Lord is at hand; it shall come as a destruction from the Almighty. Therefore shall all hands be faint, and every man's heart shall melt: And they shall be afraid; pangs and sorrows shall take hold of them; they shall be in pain as a woman that travaileth: they shall be amazed one at another; their faces shall be as flames" (vs. 6-8).

This theme is reinforced by Joel, Zephaniah, Malachi and Jeremiah. One further look should suffice (Jer. 30:5-7): "For thus saith the Lord; We have heard a voice of trembling, of fear, and not of peace. Ask ye now, and see whether a man doth travail with child? Wherefore do I see every man with his hands on his loins, as a woman in travail, and all faces are turned into paleness? Alas! for that day is great, so that none is like it: it is even the time of Jacob's trouble; but he shall be saved out of it."

Both Israel and the nations shall experience the wrath of God.

However, the principle prevails: to whom is given much, much is required. Israel enjoyed a unique advantage in terms of intimacy with God, and will be judged more severely. Increased light, opportunities and blessings are accompanied by responsibility.

As a consequence of the tribulation and judgment, souls will be revived. Wickedness will be purged, and the remnant of Israel will come to God. All things ultimately work together for good; this is the promise of the Lord for His people.

Daniel also spoke of a time of trouble such as had never been. This raised a question as to how long this period would last. In response, a celestial being answered: "...for a time, times, and an half; and when he shall have accomplished to scatter the power of the holy people, all things shall be finished" (Dan. 12:7).

In the middle of the final seven-year period, after a treaty is made, the agreement will be violated. This ushers in the violent time of tribulation. The controversy that ensues in theological circles is whether the believer is to go through this time of horror. It is our contention that scriptural precedent exists to assure us the contrary is true.

Noah was removed from judgment when the waters of the flood destroyed the earth as we knew it. Lot was taken out of harm's way when fire and brimstone were rained down from heaven to destroy Sodom and Gomorrah. Our hope is always a safe haven in such times. This would appear to be confirmed by Isaiah as well (26:20-21): "Come, my people, enter thou into thy chambers, and shut thy doors about thee: hide thyself as it were for a little moment, until the indignation be over-past. For, behold, the Lord cometh out of his place to punish the inhabitants of the earth for their iniquity: the earth also shall disclose her blood, and shall no more cover her slain."

A place of refuge has been prepared for the faithful, and they are not to be present at the time of indignation. The Lord is going to punish the wicked, but it is not the fate of him who has been justified, or covered, by the blood of the Lamb.

David similarly writes along these lines: "One thing have I

desired of the Lord, that will I seek after; that I may dwell in the house of the Lord all the days of my life, to behold the beauty of the Lord, and to inquire in His temple. For in the time of trouble he shall hide me in his pavilion: in the secret of his tabernacle shall he hide me; he shall set me up upon a rock" (Ps. 27:4-5). In Psalm 32:7, David continues to render this assurance: "Thou art my hiding place; thou shalt preserve me from trouble; thou shalt compass me about with songs of deliverance."

Some will argue that spiritual, rather than physical, refuge is offered by God, but the language suggests something much more meaningful. There will be those who are saved during the time of tribulation, so these would experience a spiritual victory. Isaiah and David, on the other hand, speak of being covered or concealed from the wrath to come.

If these passages are somewhat obscure, we can eliminate conjecture by going to the writings of the apostle Paul on this subject. In 1 Thessalonians 5:4-5, 9-11 adequate support can be found: "But ye, brethren, are not in darkness, that that day should overtake you as a thief. Ye are all children of light, and the children of the day: we are not of the night or of darkness...For God hath not appointed us to wrath, but to obtain salvation by our Lord Messiah Jesus, Who died for us, that, whether we wake or sleep, we should live together with him. Wherefore comfort yourselves together, and edify one another, even as also ye do."

All children of God are saved from the foundation of the world, and will be eternally secure. However, there are those who will be living when Jesus returns, prior to the Time of Jacob's Trouble. Being forewarned and ever watchful, these who are called children of light will be prepared. Sudden destructions will come (verse 3 of this chapter), and the unprepared will not escape.

Apparently there is a distinction. Because of that distinction, we are not appointed to wrath, or we are not to undergo that period of anguish. We therefore find solace and comfort, and are safe in Him. Frankly, the thought of having to endure the tribulation would contradict this passage. Not being removed from it would not be comforting.

We have written about the seventh trumpet that is blown on *Yom Teruah*, and commented that after a long hiatus, much starts to happen with great rapidity and surprise. The faithful await this event, but many are unprepared. That is why His coming is compared to that of a thief in the night. Chapter 4 of 1 Thessalonians bears this out (vs. 16-18): "For the Lord, himself, shall descend from heaven with a shout, with the voice of the archangel, and with the trump of God: and the dead in Messiah shall rise first: Then we who are alive and remain shall be caught up together with them in the clouds to meet the Lord in the air: and so shall we ever be with the Lord. Wherefore, comfort one another with these words."

One can only reiterate, what comfort can be found in having to endure the Tribulation? The rapture, as we refer to this meeting the Lord in the air, would seem to be totally out of context, if not for the realization that He will deliver the child of God from judgment as He did with Noah and Lot.

It is clear that all must come before the judgment seat of God to answer for the deeds performed in the body. Let us understand, however, the difference between the judgment of sin, and the rewards based upon merit. Sin has been judged in the believer. We plead the blood of Jesus, and this alone is our justification. Having been plucked out of the fire, we rejoice in His imputed righteousness. Those who have not been covered by the blood, neglecting the gift of God, are the only ones who will be judged for sin. They will be found wanting.

The judgment of the believer, on the other hand, is based upon how faithful we've been, or works. Some works are described as wood, hay and stubble. These will not endure, but our salvation in no way depends upon our works.

11

LAW OR GRACE

Traditional Jews who recognize my *Yiddishkeit*, or "Jewishness", in spite of my belief in Jesus, wonder why I do not observe the laws of *kashruth*, or keeping "*kosher*", maintaining the Sabbath, etc. Messianic Jews, who believe in Jesus but have reverted to legalistic practices, are also critical of my failure to abide by these traditions.

First, let us understand that retaining one's Jewishness does not depend upon keeping *kosher*, wearing a *yarmulke* (skullcap), *tzitzit* (fringes), etc. Ironically, the majority of my acquaintances who attend Messianic congregations or synagogues, who now wear *tallasim* (prayer shawls) and *yarmulkes*, never practiced their Judaism prior to their salvation experience. Most were non-observant Jews who suddenly feel the necessity to do what they never did before. All of a sudden, they feel compelled to display physical signs to demonstrate a relationship with God, and to use them as a testimony for unsaved Jewry.

In briefly addressing the latter point, it is conceivable that outward signs can be an encouragement to unbelieving Jews, and possibly promote harmony, or, at least, a springboard to better dialogue. However, is the price worth it?

The ends never justify the means, and our decision is to rest solely upon the Word of God. What the world deems to be success is not our goal, for the greater concern is the admonition: "Buy the truth, and sell it not" (Prov. 23:23). A greater objective is our obligation to avoid any semblance of evil.

Artificial, superficial and manufactured means of overtly being Jews do not glorify God. Conversely, what is perceived as deceit, subterfuge and surreptitious, can be most damaging and counterproductive in trying to reach the Jewish community. Most of the practices incorporated into the modern Messianic movement emanate from the synagogue, rabbinical Judaism and more modern customs, and have no Biblical foundation.

There are very real issues expressed by the unsaved Jewish community, to which we must be sensitive. The diminishing of Judaism through intermarriage, and the subsequent loss of the knowledge of Jewish traditions, are vital matters worthy of our concern. However, we cannot sacrifice truth to gain the Jews, nor are we to alienate precious Gentile believers by creating distinctions that are not meant to exist.

Solomon wrote in Ecclesiastes: "There is nothing new under the sun." What is viewed today as the Messianic movement, and which obviously is gaining momentum, is merely a resurgence of old practices. Almost twenty-five to thirty years ago, I encountered those who promoted grace and *Torah* as being synonymous. Paul, writing two thousand years ago, dealt with many of these issues. He was disturbed by the dissension promoted by the Judaizers and reprimanded those who caused this confusion (Galatians 2:14): "...If thou, being a Jew, livest after the manner of Gentiles, and not as do the Jews, why compellest thou the Gentiles to live as do the Jews?" Our goal is to determine whether we are under law or grace, and to see if there is a separate set of rules for the Gentiles.

Our starting point must be the promise of Jeremiah 31:31, which provides the foundation for our New Testament theology: "Behold, the days come, saith the Lord, that I will make a new covenant with the house of Israel, and with the house of Judah..." From this we understand that there will be a new covenant, or testament. In referring to the Old Testament, we distinguish between the gospels and epistles as opposed to the Hebrew scriptures (the Five Books of Moses, the Prophets and the Writings). Having laid the foundation for new revelation, Jeremiah continues: "Not according to the covenant that I made with their fathers in the day that I took them by the hand to bring them out of the land of Egypt; which my covenant they brake, although I was an husband unto them, saith the Lord" (v. 32).

Can there be any question as to which covenant was given at Sinai upon being brought out of Egypt? Can we deny the failure of

Israel to satisfy the requirements of that covenant? There is no other conclusion that can be drawn by any fair-minded individual. The New Covenant is to replace the *Torah*, or "Law". It is the Jew who received the Old, and it is to the Jew that the promise of the New is made.

The provisions of this new covenant relationship are outlined, beginning with verse 33: "But this shall be the covenant that I will make with the house of Israel; After those days, saith the Lord, I will put my law in their inward parts, and write it in their hearts; and will be their God, and they shall be my people. And they shall teach no more every man his neighbour, and every man his brother, saying, Know the Lord: for they shall all know me, from the least of them to the greatest of them, saith the Lord..."

In the twenty-fourth chapter of Jeremiah, God speaks of the time Israel will be replanted in the land, not to be plucked up again. At that time, He declares: "And I will give them an heart to know me, that I am the Lord: and they shall be my people, and I will be their God: for they shall return unto me with their whole heart" (v. 7).

References to this time and occasion are repeated in Ezekiel (11:19-20): "And I will give them one heart, and I will put a new spirit within you; and I will take away the stony heart out of their flesh, and I will give them an heart of flesh: That they may walk in my statutes, and keep mine ordinances, and do them: and they shall be my people, and I will be their God." He adds in 18:31: "Cast away from you all your transgressions, whereby ye have transgressed; and make a new heart and a new spirit: for why will you die, O house of Israel?" This same theme is carried through in chapter 36:24-27: "For I will take you from among the heathen, and gather you out of all countries, and will bring you into your own land. Then will I sprinkle clean water upon you, and ye shall be clean: from all your filthiness, and from all your idols, will I cleanse you. A new heart also will I give you, and a new spirit will I put within you: and I will take away the stony heart out of your flesh, and I will give you an heart of flesh. And I will put my spirit within you, and cause you to walk in my statutes, and ye shall keep my judgments, and do them."

The appraisal of the human heart was that of desperate wickedness and deceit, but a new covenant relationship with the provision of a new heart was to be the means through which truth would be internalized. A personal relationship would ensue between man and his Creator.

In Hebrews chapter 8, the writer of the epistle quotes from Jeremiah 31 and comments: "For if that first covenant had been faultless, then should no place have been sought for the second...In that He saith, A new covenant, He hath made the first old. Now that which decayeth and waxeth old is ready to vanish away" (vs. 7, 13). Thus groundwork is laid to recognize a distinction between law and grace. None of this suggests harmony between the two.

The Old Testament was sanctified by the blood shed upon the altar, so the writer is careful to explain in Heb. 9:13-14: "For if the blood of bulls and of goats, and the ashes of an heifer sprinkling the unclean, sanctifieth to the purifying of the flesh: How much more shall the blood of Messiah, who through the eternal Spirit offered himself without spot to God, purge your conscience from dead works to serve the living God?"

Jesus, then, is the mediator of the New Testament, but: "...where a testament is, there must also of necessity be the death of the testator. For a testament is of force after men are dead: otherwise it is of no strength at all while the testator liveth" (vs. 16-17).

Hebrews chapter 10 goes on to explain that the Law (the Old Covenant) was the shadow of things to come; a means of preparing our understanding for the role of Jesus, the Lamb of God, Who takes away the sin of the world. Quoting from Psalm 40:7-8, verses 7, 9-10 of Hebrews reveals that God had no pleasure in the sacrificial system, but it paved the way for the ultimate sacrifice: "Then said I, Lo, I come (in the volume of the book it is written of me,) to do thy will, O God...He taketh away the first, that He may establish the second. By the which will we are sanctified through the offering of the body of Messiah Jesus once for all."

The covenant of the law had to be satisfied before the new covenant of grace could be established. Once the old was fulfilled, however, the new took effect. The two could never co-exist. *Torah* and grace are diametrically opposed. Either justification comes from the Law, or by faith in Him Who imputes His righteousness unto the unworthy.

Remember the difference: "This is the covenant that I will make with them after those days, saith the Lord, I will put my laws into their hearts, and in their minds will I write them..." (v. 16). The Law was holy and perfect and just, but it had no power to change a man. Our propensity to sin and violate the Law dishonored God, and steps had to be taken to empower us to live by God's standards.

The Law is called the schoolmaster that brought us to Messiah. It revealed our weakness and needs, but changed nothing. It exposed the futility of keeping the ordinances and manifested a need that only God could meet.

In developing this point, Paul, in Romans 3:1 asks rhetorically, "What advantage then hath the Jew?" Per Romans 3:2: "Much every way: chiefly, because that unto them were committed the oracles of God." But inasmuch as all of them have sinned, all are guilty under the Law, and, according to verse 20, "Therefore by the deeds of the law there shall no flesh be satisfied in his sight: for by the law is the knowledge of sin."

Most importantly then: "Therefore we conclude that a man is justified by faith without the deeds of the law (v. 28). Paul then adds that the God of the Jew and the Gentile justifies both through faith. However, the Law is not made void by faith, but is rather established by faith.

In essence, we are no longer bound by the Law, but a new relationship has evolved whereby a new heart and new spirit act as a catalyst to surrender the will to God. His taking control of the life of an obedient child is the means through which the perfect will of God is accomplished. Legalism becomes a thing of the past.

A yielded life is not one of Do's and Don't's, but a heart responding out of love. Being crucified with Jesus is the means through which we serve Him, and not self, or sin. Sin, then, has no dominion over us, for we are now under grace (Rom. 6:14).

Romans 7 draws an analogy by distinguishing between a married woman and a widow. Responsibility to a husband, he says, ceases with his demise. In like manner we become dead to the Law, "...that we should serve in newness of the spirit, and not in the oldness of the letter" (v .6). "For the law of the Spirit of life in Messiah Jesus hath made me free from the law of sin and death...Therefore, brethren, we are debtors, not to the flesh, to live after the flesh" (vs. 8:2, 12).

The teaching that has become popular today is that the Law has no application to the Gentiles, who are the ones addressed in this epistle to the Romans. This distinction allegedly is supported by Galatians 2:7, where Paul comments: "...the gospel of the uncircumcision was committed unto me, as the gospel of the circumcision was unto Peter..." We are then to conclude that two gospels exist; one for the Jew and one for the Gentile. Is this, however, in any way supported by the facts?

Conversely, Paul reprimands those who distinguish between Jew and Gentile. His admonition is clear: "Knowing that a man is not justified by the works of the law, but the faith of Messiah Jesus, even we have believed in Messiah Jesus, that we might be justified by the faith of Messiah, and not by the works of the law: for by the works of the law shall no flesh be justified" (Gal. 2:16). In other words, there is only one gospel, but Paul and Peter were called to different roles in bringing this truth to two different audiences.

In declaring that no flesh can be justified by the Law, we must always remember that a Jew who returns to the Law has already been justified by the atonement in Jesus. The Law could not bring him into that relationship. On the other hand: "For if I build again the things which I destroyed, I make myself a transgressor (v. 18). Returning to the Law, and living in the flesh, only creates the possibility to fail all over again. Paul therefore proclaims: "I do not frustrate the grace of God: for if righteousness come by the law, then Messiah is dead in vain" (v. 21). Paul goes on to challenge the readers of his epistle (3:3): "Are ye so foolish? having begun in the Spirit, are ye now made perfect by the flesh?" Those of us who have been justified by the death of Jesus must respond to this question. Is the return to the Law in actuality a prideful manifestation of negating the dependency we have on what Jesus accomplished in His death?

We must consider: "For as many as are of the works of the law are under the curse...But that no man is justified by the law in the sight of God, it is evident: for, The just shall live by faith. And the law is not of faith..." (vs. 10-12).

If we consider the Law "...was added because of transgressions, till the seed should come to whom the promise was made..." (v. 19), we will have accomplished much. The point being made is that there would be an end to the Law upon the appearance of Jesus and His fulfillment thereof ("till the seed should come"). The *zerah shel eshah*, the "seed of the woman", the promised Messiah from the predicted virgin birth, had come. The purpose of the Law has been served; and we see Jesus as our righteousness. It is not our keeping of the Law.

Pay careful attention, then, to Galatians 3:23-25: "But before faith came, we were kept under the law, shut up unto the faith which should afterwards be revealed. Wherefore the law was our schoolmaster to bring us unto Messiah, that we might be justified by faith. But after that faith is come, we are no longer under a schoolmaster."

Here again, the attempt to distinguish between Jew and Gentile is refuted by verse 28: "There is neither Jew nor Greek, there is neither bond nor free, their is neither male nor female: for ye are all one in Messiah Jesus." How sad that some would rebuild the wall of partition between Jew and Gentile, that had been torn down by Jesus. There is no foundation for the teaching that there are two gospels, for God is no respecter of persons, and no such distinction exists.

Keeping *kosher*, according to some Messianic congregations, is essential. They claim Peter's vision of the four-cornered sheet (Acts 10:9ff), with all manner of creeping things and beasts, had nothing to do with eliminating the laws of *kashruth* (keeping kosher). The object lesson was to show that God cleansed the Gentile as well as the Jew. However, when this vision was given to Peter, the message was: "...What God hath cleansed, that call not thou common" (v. 15). It was the creeping things that were formerly forbidden, but now abstinence was no longer mandatory. Paul wrote as well, in Gal. 4:9, 21: "But now, after that ye have known God, or rather are known of God, how turn ye again to the weak and beggarly elements, whereunto ye desire again to be in bondage?...Tell me, ye that desire to be under the law, do ye hear the law?"

Using the analogy of Abraham's two sons, one born of a freewoman (Sarah), and the other by a bondslave (Hagar), he explains that we are the children of promise. Having been set free, we are not the offspring of the slave, and not to be entangled again with the yoke of bondage (the Law). "Messiah is become of no effect unto you, whosoever of you are justified by the law; ye are fallen from grace" (Gal. 5:4). No matter how one protests that he is justified by grace, but insists the Law must be kept, can these opposing points be reconciled. No semantics can camouflage the inherent contradiction of terms. Being a Jew, or a better Jew, will never result from works or the circumcision of the flesh. Claiming distinctions between Jewish and Gentile believers, likewise, will never be supported by the Word of God.

Paul addresses the issue of *kashruth* in 1 Corinthians 10. He makes it clear that: "All things are lawful for me..." (v. 23); and, "...if I by grace be a partaker, why am I evil spoken of for that for which I give thanks? Whether therefore ye eat, or drink, or whatsoever ye do, do all to the glory of God" (v. 30).

My wife and I maintained a *kosher* home prior to our salvation experience, and we continued for a period of time after. Reading the Word of God brought me to understand that I followed a tradition. I continued with a prideful attitude, deeming that I was a better example for having undertaken such an obligation, which reasserted my Jewishness.

One day I was confronted by Romans 14:2-3, 5-6, and was challenged to reconsider my motivation: "For one believeth that he may eat all things: another, who is weak, eateth herbs. Let not him that eateth despise him that eateth not; and let not him which eateth not judge him that eateth: for God hath received him...One man esteemeth one day above another: another esteemeth every day alike. Let every man be fully persuaded in his own mind. He that regardeth the day, regardeth it unto the Lord; and he that regardeth not the day, to the Lord he doth not regard it. He that eateth, eateth to the Lord, for he giveth God thanks; and he that eateth not, to the Lord he eateth not, and giveth God thanks."

To those of you who, in good conscience, cannot share the conclusions to which I have come, I do not sit in judgment. I pray, however, that the true motivation of the heart will be searched out. Regardless of which choice one makes for himself, the greater concern is the teaching and emphasis of those ministries which invoke a yoke of bondage upon those who would never come to such a conclusion (reverting to the Law) on their own. It is not appropriate to create an obligation where none exists, and it is certainly not right to encourage separatism, legalism or dissension.

EPILOGUE

It is our sincere desire that the material presented here gives you a better understanding of the Jewish people, and admiration for the role they have played in God's plan to reach all with the gospel. Perhaps it will awaken renewed fervor and compassion for the lost sheep of the house of Israel. While it may not be easy to present the gospel to most Jewish people, a loving heart, fortified by knowledge of the Hebrew scriptures, will help plant the seed.

Saving souls is the work of the Lord, and none of us have that responsibility. However, since faith comes by the hearing of the Word, we realize that God uses us in the process. Regardless of how frustrating it may seem, our faithfulness in serving our purpose will be enhanced by maintaining a proper perspective. In a final attempt to close on such a note, it may help to recall an incident in the life of King David. He is a picture of Messiah in many ways, so the application should be fairly obvious. David was beloved of his father, came from means, and was anointed as king at an early age. In spite of this, he spent years in hiding and obscurity. King Saul wanted to kill him, and most of David's early years were spent in fleeing for his life. David's own children rebelled against him and sought to dethrone him. Absalom turned the hearts of the nation against his father. *Av Shalom* is the Hebrew for "Father of Peace". Even as Satan comes as an angel of light, this pretender to the throne wanted to overcome God's anointed. Yet David still loved and mourned for his son, and desired that no harm come to him. What a figure of a merciful Redeemer Who forgives and desires that none perish!

David was not only an innocent sufferer, he endured his lot in silence. Nothing is recorded to suggest that he became bitter, angry or complaining. His confidence was in the Lord, and his psalms stand as a testimony to a relationship of trust, confidence and love. He best personifies Messiah, in his submission, as stated in Ps. 40:7-8: "Then said I, Lo, I come: in the volume of the book it is written of me, I delight to do thy will, O my God: yea, thy law is written in my heart."

The trials of David's life never caused him to turn from God. Years in the wilderness, being hunted like an animal, the loss of four sons and ultimately the failure of his health, did not diminish his enthusiasm for God. His obedience, enthusiasm and desire to live righteously should serve as an example for us in dealing with the unsaved. After the death of Saul and Jonathan, David inquired if there were anyone left from the house of Saul to whom he could show kindness. The response was that Jonathan's son, Mephibosheth, dwelled in the land of *Lo Debar*.

2 Samuel chapter 4 records that Mephibosheth was only five years old when Jonathan was slain in battle. His nurse snatched him up to flee, fearing that David would seek vengeance upon the descendants of Saul. In her haste, she dropped the lad, and he became a cripple for life.

When David sent for Mephibosheth and brought him to the palace, he invited him to dine at his table continually. The king of Israel offered continual protection and sustenance to the lame man, but Mephibosheth didn't trust David. All he knew was that he was physically impaired for life, and David was the one responsible.

I can identify with Mephibosheth. His name in Hebrew means "to scatter shame or confusion". He was dwelling in the land of *Lo Debar*, the Hebrew compound of "No Word". Confusion ensues when there is a lack of the Word of God. After hearing only bad things, and then being handicapped for life, it was not easy for Mephibosheth to trust the one deemed to be responsible.

In the name of Jesus, Jews, as myself, have been persecuted and tormented. Most of us have lived in *Lo Debar*: without the benefit of the Word. We have been in confusion as to the truth of the gospel, and not knowing our Messiah. Consequently, when we finally hear the Word, there is distrust and suspicion.

The Lord has made eternal provision (to eat at His table continually), but this truth is not readily understood. Are we as willing as David to come and do the will of God? Are we ready to withstand rejection and distrust, understanding the basis for the confusion?

Many of our Jewish brothers and sisters are still in *Lo Debar*. They will remain there as long as we fail to reach out in love, in spite of possible rejection. Before making that decision, think what would have been had not someone reached out to you.

Hungering and thirsting for the righteousness of God is necessary for each of us to respond to His call. I pray that He will open your eyes to this high calling, and give you a desire to impart this fervor to those who remain in darkness.

> O God, thou art my God; early will I seek thee: my soul thirsteth for thee, my flesh longeth for thee in a dry and thirsty land, where no water is; To see thy power and thy glory, so as I have seen thee in the sancturary. Because thy lovingkindness is better than life, my lips shall praise thee. Thus will I bless thee while I live: I will lift up my hands in thy name. My soul shall be satisfied as with marrow and fatness; and my mouth shall praise thee with joyful lips: When I remember thee upon my bed, and meditate on thee in the night watches. Because thou hast been my help, therefore in the shadow of thy wings will I rejoice" (Ps. 63:1-7).

GLOSSARY

Absalom;
Av-shalom: — "father of peace" (son of David)
Adonoi: — Lord (frequently used instead of using the sacred name of Jehovah)
afikomen: — middle matzah used in Passover matzah tash; Greek for "He is risen" (something no longer present)
Akiva: — famous Jewish rabbi who started Yeshiva academies in B'nai B'rak; supporter of false messiah, Bar Cochba
almah: — virgin; routinely translated as "young woman" in Hebrew scriptures
ammi: — my people
Avi Ad: — Hebrew for "Everlasting Father"
barah: — created
bar: — son (feminine, *bas*, "daughter")
Bar Cochba: — messianic pretender and military leader
Bar Mitzvah: — "son of commandment'; religious service when son comes of age, usually at thirteen
Bethlehem;
Bet-lechem: — House of Bread
bethulah: — Hebrew word usually translated as "virgin"; young woman of marriageable age
bikkurim: — firstfruits (offering of harvest)
bitzah: — hard-boiled egg used on Seder plate to symbolize the free-will offering used while the Temple stood
Boaz: — King David's grandfather; Hebrew for "strength"
Brit Chadasha: — Hebrew for "New Testament", or covenant
Brit mi'lah: — covenant of circumcision
B'reishis: — Hebrew for "In the beginning", the opening word of the Bible (Genesis)
carpas: — parsley used on Seder plate to remind one of a spring festival; also symbolic of hyssop

caw-ari:	– Hebrew for "like a lion"
chalal:	– Hebrew for "bore", "pierced" or "wounded"
Chanukkah:	– dedication, "Festival of Lights"
charoses:	– mixture of chopped apples, nuts and wine used on Seder plate to symbolize the mortar used by the Hebrew slaves in Egypt
Chasidim:	– literally, "Saints", a strict sect of Orthodox Jewish people
chaver:	– friend, companion, stripes or wounds
chometz:	– anything made with leaven, not *kosher* for Passover
dacah:	– Hebrew for "crushed", or "to grind to powder"
Diaspora:	– Dispersion - the forced scattering of the Jewish nation due to persecution
dreidel	– a small top played with during *Chanukah*
echad:	– Hebrew for "compound one", expresses unity
El:	– Hebrew singular for "God"
El Gibbor:	– Mighty God
Elimelech:	– husband of Naomi; Hebrew for "My God is King"
Eloheinu:	– "Our God", plural form, literally "Gods"
Emuneh:	– Faithful
Ephraim:	– son of Joseph, literally "fruitful"
goel:	– "kinsman-redeemer", near relative
goy:	– "nation", "non-Jew" (plural, *goyim*)
hallel:	– Hebrew for "praise", the title given to Psalms 113-118
haftorah:	– portion of scripture from the prophets used in the weekly reading in synagogue on the Sabbath
haggadah:	– Hebrew for "the narration" or "the telling", a book of readings and songs, and an order of service, recounting God's miraculous intervention in freeing the Jewish people from bondage in Egypt
hineh:	– Hebrew for "behold", introduces important thought
Hoshanna Rabbah:	– "The Great Salvation", part of Succos and linked to water libation

Immanuel:	– "God with us"; name for Messiah (Is. 7:14)
Jeconiah:	– Also *Coniah*, king of Judah upon whom a curse was invoked by God (Jer. 22:24)
Jehovah:	– Name of God; "The Eternal", or the "I Am"
Jehovah Tzitkenu:	– "The Lord our Righteousness"
Jerusalem:	– the "City of Peace"
Jeshurun:	– poetic name for Israel (Deut. 32:15, Is. 44:2)
kashruth:	– observance of the tenets of the Mosaic Law
kipporah:	– Hebrew for "covering", or "atonement", (from the root *kaper*)
kosher:	– observance of the Mosaic and/or rabbinical dietary laws
Lag B'omer:	– The 33rd day of the counting of the *omer* (during the days of counting between Passover and Shavuos)
Lo Ammi:	– son of Hosea; literally "not my people"
Lo Ruchamah:	– son of Hosea; literally "not pitied"
Marah:	– another name of Naomi, literally "bitter"
matzah:	– unleavened bread
matzah tash:	– linen container with three compartments to house three slices of matzah on Seder table
megilla:	– book or scroll
melech:	– king
Melech ha Olam:	– "King of the Universe"; God
menorah:	– a seven-branched candelabra, designed by God for the Tabernacle and Temple – adopted by the state of Israel as its national symbol. A nine-branched *menorah*, used in the celebration of *Chanukah*, is referred to as a *Chanukah menorah* or *chanukiah*
Mephibosheth:	– son of Jonathan; literally "scatterer of shame or confusion"
meshummed:	– Hebrew for "traitor to the faith"

Messiah:	– English equivalent of *Moshiach* or "Anointed One"
mezuzah:	– container on doorposts housing portions of scripture from Deuteronomy and Exodus
Midrash:	– rabbinical commentary on Talmud passage (exposition on prophetic writings; from root *drash*, "to search out")
Mishcan:	– "Tabernacle"
mitzvah:	– "deed", or "commandment"
Mitzraim:	– Egypt, literally "double strait", or "narrow"
molech:	– "angel" or "messenger"
Molech ha Maves:	– "Angel of Death"
moror:	– horseradish used on Passover Seder plate; literally "bitter", to symbolize the bitterness of the Israelites' bondage in Egypt
Moshiach:	– Hebrew for "Messiah" (Greek *Christ*)
natzal:	– spoil, snatch or pluck
nazah:	– to sprinkle (in expiation)
nishku bar:	– "pay homage to", or "kiss", "the son"
or lagoyim:	– "light to the nations"
os:	– "sign" or "miracle" (alternative, *ot*)
Otot ha Moshiach:	– apocalyptic midrash, literally "Signs of the Messiah"
ovair:	– to "cross over", or "be in opposition"
Pesach:	– Passover; literally "exempt"
pogrom:	– organized persecution with intent to annihilate
Purim:	– (Festival of) Lots
rabbi:	– "teacher"
retzuot:	– leather straps to bind *t'phillin*
Rosh Hashanna:	– Jewish New Year; literally "head of the year"
Sar Shalom:	– name ascribed to Messiah (Is. 9:6); literally "Prince of Peace"
Septuagint:	– Greek translation of the Bible (named for 70 rabbis

shachan:	who did the translation) - "dwelling place"; feminine - *shachana*
Shalom Aleichem:	- Peace be with you (typical Hebrew greeting)
Shavuos:	- "Feast of Weeks" or "Pentecost"
Shekina:	- "God's glory", referenced above - residence of God's glory or radiance
shevah:	- Hebrew for "seven"
Shiloh:	- name for Messiah (Ge. 49:10); city north of Bethel; from Hebrew *shalom* or "peace"
Shlosh Raglaim:	- "three pilgrimage festivals" (Passover, Shavuos and Succos)
Sh'ma:	- profession of faith in the unity of God; literally "hear"
Shmini Atzeret:	- conclusion festival of Succos; eighth day of assembly
shofar:	- ram's horn, blown as a signal (for important occasions, assemblies, etc.)
siddur:	- Hebrew prayer book
Succos:	- "Festival of Booths", or "Tabernacles"
tallis:	- prayer shawl with fringes
Tanas Esther:	- the "Fast of Esther"
targum:	- expository writing
Tisha B'Av:	- the ninth day of the Hebrew month, *Av* (commemorating the destruction of both Temples)
Tishrei:	- the seventh month of the Hebrew calendar
T'Nach:	- Hebrew Bible; from T=*Torah* (law), N=*N'viim* (prophets), C=*C'tuvim* (writings)
t'phillin:	- phylacteries; small cases with scripture, to be bound on arm and forehead for morning prayers
t'shuveh:	- repentance; to turn around spiritually
tzadik:	- "righteous one"
tzedek:	- "righteousness"
tzitzit:	- "fringes" (alternative, *tzitsis*)
Vayeishev:	- Hebrew for "And he lived"

yachid:	-Hebrew for "absolute one"
Yamim Nora'im:	-Days of Awe
Yeshua:	-Hebrew name for Jesus; literally "salvation"
yetzer harah:	-"evil nature"
yetzer tov:	-"good nature"
Yom Haatzmuot:	-Day of Independence
Yom Kippor:	-Day of Atonement
Yom Teruah:	-Day of the Sounding of the Alarm
Yom Yerushalayim:	- Jerusalem Day (Day of the City of Peace)
yonek:	-"small shoot", or "suckling child"
zerah shel eshah:	-"seed of woman"
Zion:	-name for Jerusalem or Israel
Zohar:	-Hebrew mystical writing
z'roah:	-the roasted lamb shankbone on the Passover Seder plate, symbolizing the lamb sacrificed on Passover

ABOUT THE AUTHOR

Born and raised in the Bronx, NY, Martin Fromm attended DeWitt Clinton High School, and then earned a BBA from the Bernard M. Baruch School of Business and Public Administration. He served in the U.S. Army in Orleans and Poitiers, France. As a Chaplain's Assistant to the Rabbi ministering to the Southeast sector, Martin was a liaison to the French Jewish community.

For the past thirty years, he has been teaching the scriptures throughout the United States, and conducting home Bible studies. His primary goal is to promote understanding of the Jewish contribution in preparing, presenting and promulgating the Word of God.

Martin is the president of the American Messianic Mission, Inc., a Hebrew-Christian outreach and fellowship with branches in North Lauderdale, Florida and Floral Park, New York.

He and Judy, his wife of thirty-five years, reside in Bayside, NY.